Exeter Medieval English Texts and Studies
General Editors: Marion Glasscoe and M. J. Swanton

T0341411

ÆLFRIC

LIVES OF THREE ENGLISH SAINTS

Edited by

G. I. NEEDHAM

UNIVERSITY
of
EXETER
PRESS

First published in Methuen's Old English Library,
London, 1966

This revised edition published by University of Exeter Press
in 1976 and reprinted 1992

University of Exeter Press
Reed Hall, Streatham Drive
Exeter EX4 4QR
UK
www.exeterpress.co.uk

Printed digitally since 2001

ISBN 978 0 85989 076 2

Printed and bound by CPI Group (UK) Ltd, Croydon, CR0 4YY

CONTENTS

ABBREVIATIONS

ÆLFRIC: LIVES OF THREE ENGLISH SAINTS

NED	*New English Dictionary*
OE	Old English
Plummer II . . .	C. Plummer, *Ven. Baedae Opera Historica*, vol. II, 1896
Plummer ii . . .	C. Plummer, *Two of the Saxon Chronicles Parallel*, vol. II, 1899
Primer	*Sweet's Anglo-Saxon Primer*, 9th ed., revised by Norman Davis, 1953
QW	Randolph Quirk and C. L. Wrenn, *An Old English Grammar*, 1955
RES	*Review of English Studies*
rev	reviser (see p. 1, fn. 2)
RS	Rolls Series
s.a.	*sub anno*
SB	*Altenglische Grammatik nach der Angelsächsischen Grammatik von Eduard Sievers*, neubearb. von Karl Brunner, 1942
Schrader . . .	B. Schrader, *Studien zur Ælfricschen Syntax*, 1887
Sisam, *Studies* . .	K. Sisam, *Studies in the History of Old English Ltierature*, 1953
SP	*Studies in Philology*
Stenton	F. M. Stenton, *Anglo-Saxon England*, 1943
TRHS	*Transactions of the Royal Historical Society*
WS	West Saxon

INTRODUCTION

I. MANUSCRIPTS

THE homilies printed in this volume are preserved in the following manuscripts:[1]

MS A, British Museum MS, Cotton Julius E VII (Ker, No. 162), of the beginning of the eleventh century, which consists for the most part of a course of homilies for holy days, chiefly saints' days, arranged in the order of the church year.[2]

MS B, Bodleian MS 343 (Ker, No. 310), of the second half of the twelfth century, a large collection of homilies, including many by Ælfric.

MS G, Gloucester Cathedral MS 35 (Ker, No. 117), consisting of fragments recovered from bindings: three of the leaves, in

---

[1] I have used the same sigla for the manuscripts as Skeat (see next footnote). I give Ker's date in all cases.

[2] Ed. W. W. Skeat, *Ælfric's Lives of Saints* (E.E.T.S., O.S. 76, 82, 94, 114) (1881–1900), with variant readings from the other MSS (but see below, p. 4, fn. 5, and p. 6, fn. 1). Skeat does not print the last two items in the MS, which are by Ælfric, but stand outside the annual cycle (see also below, p. 2, fn. 4). The homilies in this volume are nos. XXVI (*St Oswald*), XXXII (*St Edmund*) and XXI (*St Swithin*) in Skeat's edition.

Additions and alterations have been made by an almost contemporary reviser to a number of the homilies in this MS (including the three printed here). Many of them are of a purely linguistic nature, and are referred to in section III below. Those which affect the sense, though supported in a few instances by the other MSS, appear in general to have no textual authority: none of them is very extensive, and few are of more than minor importance.

In what follows, the expression 'MS A' is to be understood as referring to the MS in its original state, before it was worked on by the reviser, except that, where letters have been erased from the MS, it refers to the present state of the MS (since it is obviously impossible to be certain whether an erasure was made by the reviser or the original scribe). All the reviser's alterations are recorded in the textual notes. See also RES NS ix (1958) 160–4.

a hand of the first half of the eleventh century, contain parts of the homily on St Swithin.

MS O, British Museum MS, Cotton Otho B X (Ker, No. 177A), of the first half of the eleventh century, seriously damaged in the fire of 1731.[1] This part of what was probably originally a composite MS, contained chiefly lives of saints, most of them by Ælfric, including ten of the lives in MS A.[2]

MS U, University Library, Cambridge, MS Ii. 1. 33 (Ker, No. 18), of the second half of the twelfth century, a collection chiefly of lives of saints, most of them by Ælfric, fifteen of them corresponding with homilies by him in MS A.[3] The MS also contains the sole surviving copy of Ælfric's homily for the feast of St Vincent.[4]

MS V, British Museum MS, Cotton Vitellius D XVII (Ker, No. 222), of the middle of the eleventh century, seriously damaged in the fire of 1731;[5] a large collection of lives of saints, almost all of them by Ælfric, twenty of them corresponding with homilies by him in MS A,[6] and twenty-seven with homilies by him in MS U.

II. TEXT

Differences between the manuscripts affecting sense, grammar, syntax or style, are fairly numerous, though seldom very important. The variants rarely offer a simple choice between a possible and an impossible, or even a less possible, reading: corruption would rarely be suspected if

[1] Where readings from the damaged MSS O and V are given, letters no longer present, or totally illegible, are printed in square brackets, letters imperfectly legible in round brackets.

[2] Ker, arts. 10, 12, 13 correspond to Skeat nos. XXXIII, XXIIIB, and XXIII, which are not by Ælfric.

[3] Including the homily *De Falsis Diis*, not printed by Skeat (see above, p. 1, fn. 2).

[4] Ker, art. 23, printed by Skeat ii 426-42 (no. XXXVII).

[5] See fn. 1 above.

[6] Ker, art. 29, corresponds to Skeat no. XXX, which is not by Ælfric.

there were no variants to draw attention to it.[1] This is true
not only of alterations which are probably due to deliberate
scribal interference, but also of those which appear to be,
at least partly, accidental, e.g. II 85, *here* BU (*hæse* A),
III 309 f, lacuna in A. Consequently, where other criteria
are lacking, it is difficult, sometimes impossible, to say with
certainty which variant preserves the author's original, and
which the copyists' alteration of it.[2] This is particularly true
of variants affecting the word-order; none of them, however,
is of more than slight importance. The highest proportion of
variants involves omissions from, or additions to, the text.
It appears from those instances (the great majority) where
originality can be established with reasonable certainty, that
omissions occur almost twice as often as additions. Omis-
sions vary considerably in importance; additions are almost
all of minor words, superfluous conjunctions, pronouns,
intensifying adverbs, etc. Next in frequency come sub-
stitutions of words similar in meaning, or form, or both.
Such substitutions do not often greatly affect the sense,
though they sometimes spoil the alliteration, and they are
very seldom completely implausible. From the frequency
with which inferior readings of all kinds occur in the various
MSS, MSS A and G appear to be the most reliable, B, U, and
V the least. Inferior readings in A and O appear most often
to be accidental, in G and particularly in U, to be due to
deliberate 'improvement'; B is full of alterations, both
accidental and deliberate.

St Oswald: two complete copies are preserved, in A,
ff. 153^r–157^v (Ker, art. 37), and in U, ff. 161^r–166^r (Ker,
art. 31); ll. 130 ([*genealæh*]*ton*) to 195 (*moldan*) are preserved
fairly complete in V, f. 10^{r-v} (Ker, art. 31). The text in U
differs in a number of places from that in A, and, where
readings are available, from that in V also. In most instances
A, or AV, have the better reading; occasionally, however,
the reading in U is to be preferred, and the probably

---

[1] This is less true of B than of the other MSS.

[2] In such cases the reading of the base-text (see below, p. 6) has
been allowed to stand.

inferior variant shared by AV at l. 152 may indicate a genetic relationship between them.[1] Certainly the remaining variants offer no evidence to conflict with this: there are no certainly inferior readings common to AU[2] or UV.[3]

St Edmund: two complete copies are preserved, in A, ff. 203ʳ–207ʳ (Ker, art. 43), and B, ff. 62ʳ–64ʳ (Ker, art. 31);[4] there is a third text of l. 14 to the end in U, ff. 151ʳ–155ᵛ (Ker, art. 29); l. 203 (ðo(*n*)e *martyr*) to the end (only partly legible) is preserved in V, f. 79ʳ (Ker, art. 42), and ll. 1–161 (*halidom*[*e*]) (again only partly legible) in O, ff. 42ʳ–44ᵛ (Ker, art. 21).[5] There are a number of inferior readings common to BO,[6] suggesting a genetic relationship between them. Although B has many inferior readings not in O, O has only one not in B: 79 *hælendum* OU, (*hælende*

---

[1] The spelling *Bardanige* l. 148 shared by AV (*Beardanige* U) tends to confirm this: Bede has *Beardaneu*, and the first element is *Beardan-* (or *Bearðan-*) invariably in Chron. (all MSS, except in the late interpolation in E 675, which has *Barþanig*). The relationship would be certain if it could be established that the original reading of A at l. 165 was *wohnysse* as in V (cp textual notes); but the erasure has been carried out very efficiently. Cp also ll. 152n, 174n.

[2] Possible examples occur at ll. 138, 183; at l. 135, V has the inferior reading.

[3] The only common variant is *wegferende* l. 169 (*wegfarende* A). From BT it appears that the form *wegfarende* is very rare (LS XXXI 992, and Napier 192/23 are the only other examples; at LS XXVIII 154, also quoted, the MS has *wegfærende*); while *wegferende* is common, and occurs a number of times in CH (as printed by Thorpe); but I do not know the extent of MS support for it there. If it were not for this reading, V might be taken to be a copy of A.

[4] Ed. Benjamin Thorpe, *Analecta Anglo-Saxonica* (2nd ed. 1846) 119–26. Thorpe's text is quite accurate, but the following errors should be noted: 122/26 *sæcgæð hit:* MS *hit sæcgæð*; 123/5 *willunge:* MS *wissunge*; 123/18 *on tune:* MS *to tune*; 123/32 *wundæ:* MS *wundræ*; 124/11 *þeofæs:* MS *þeowæs*; 124/33 *he reowsode:* MS (probably) *bereowsode*; a few words have been omitted at the end (see l. 228 textual notes); and there are about a dozen minor orthographic errors.

[5] Skeat gives few collations from this copy (see vol. ii, p. xvii).

[6] Inferior readings in B are extremely common: readings are available from O in 29 instances (slightly less than half), and agree with B's inferior reading five times (ll. 24, 119 f, 121, 139, 144).

AB);[1] but the inferior reading may clearly have arisen independently in OU. Furthermore the appearance of the better reading in B may equally well be fortuitous, since the scribe of B, in modernizing the language, frequently changes *-um* to *-e*. It follows that B could be a copy of O. There are a considerable number of places where U differs from A. In relatively few cases is it possible to decide with confidence which preserves the better reading. A's agreements with B and (where extant) O, are about equal in number to those of U.[2] There appear to be no inferior readings in the first category,[3] and only one in the second: 85 *here* BU, (*hæse* A), which could have arisen independently.[4] The possibility, however, remains that it, and other variants shared by U with BO, are derived from a common source. There are no certainly inferior readings common to AU.[5] The small fragment preserved in V contains a number of inferior readings,[6] but only one in common with another MS: 228 *and lof* BV, (om. AU), and this commonplace elaboration of the doxology (particularly liable to such treatment), is probably of no significance.

St Swithin: is preserved entire only in A, ff. 96ᵛ–103ʳ (Ker, art. 27); ll. 16 (*and oferworht*) to 135 (*se*), and 315 (*hwæt*) to 373 (*sibbe*) are preserved in G, ff. 1ʳ–3ᵛ (Ker, art. 1);[7] and l. 13 (*him*) to the end (only partly legible) in O,

---

[1] The word *hælend* normally has substantival inflection (for the dat. cp I 210, II 96): there are indications elsewhere of a tendency to substitute adjectival inflection in the dat. (e.g. LS XXIV 18).

[2] At l. 74 B differs from both, and at l. 164 no reading from B is available.

[3] At ll. 43, 103, 113, 190 U clearly has the inferior reading; at ll. 87, 91 f, 124, 139, 178, 190, 219 the variants appear to be of equal merit.

[4] Possibly also 186 f (see notes), which could also, though less probably, have arisen independently in BU. At ll. 49, 119 f clearly, and at ll. 132, 175 probably, A has the inferior reading; at ll. 36, 39, 40 f, 113, 148, 149 the variants appear to be of equal merit.

[5] Possible examples occur at ll. 47, 75, 211, 214, 222.

[6] ll. 207, 217, 222.

[7] Photozincographic facsimiles of the three leaves were published by John Earle in *Gloucester Fragments* (1861), which also contains

ff. 37^r–42^r (Ker, art. 20).[1] Inferior readings occur in all three MSS, but none is shared by any two of them.[2]

The present edition of the three homilies is presented in the form of a corrected base-text. MS A has been chosen as the base-text of all three homilies for the following reasons: the texts preserved in MSS GOV are fragmentary; MS U, which preserves complete texts of *St Oswald* and *St Edmund*, would from a textual point of view, have provided a possible alternative base-text for these two homilies, but is less acceptable than MS A from a linguistic point of view;[3] finally, the textual and linguistic character of MS B,[3] which preserves a complete copy of *St Edmund*, clearly makes the choice of it as a base-text for that homily impossible.

III. LANGUAGE

The normal linguistic usage of MSS AGOUV is in all important respects identical. Departures from the normal usage of the group are fewest in G; in A, on which this edition is based, they are rather numerous; in U, despite its late date, they are not much more numerous than in A.[4] It seems likely that the normal usage of this group of MSS—

'An Essay on the Life and Times of St Swithun', and much valuable illustrative material. The facsimile is on the whole quite good, except at a few points, the most important of which are: 4/19 *nan* altered from *man* by erasure; Y/18 *h* erased before *raðe*; Y/30 read *bedydrian*: the letters *dy* have faded; in addition, many accents have not come out clearly, or in some cases at all. Skeat's collations were made from the facsimile (see vol. i, p. 552).

[1] Skeat gives no collations from this copy (see vol. ii, p. xvi).

[2] Variants shared by GO of equal merit with those in A occur at ll. 70, 317, 326, 366; similar neutral variants shared by AO at ll. 36, 37; and by AG at ll. 126, 337.

[3] On the linguistic character of MSS B and U, see next section.

[4] The late date of U is reflected in a number of features, all paralleled in the modernizations introduced by the scribe of B, e.g. the occasional spelling *u* for LWS *ȳ*, due to French orthographic influence; the occasional loss of final *n* in inflections; occasional syncopated forms *cyng*, *king*; and the occasional substitution of *ðe* for *se* (dem.adj. and rel.pron.).

typically LWS—represents fairly closely that of the author; but to what extent this is true in detail, it is impossible to say, since so few complete and reliable descriptions of the language of these and other MSS of Ælfric's works are at present available. In the present edition the linguistic forms of the base-text, MS A, have been retained, and no attempt has been made to normalize them. Some of the features of the normal usage of the group, and some of the deviations which occur, are considered in this section.[1]

There are occasional instances of *e* for *ǽ* in A, e.g. *fec* III 130, and for *ǣ*, e.g. *geemtigod* III 233, *het* (3 sg. pres. ind.) II 45, III 31, *genealecan* I 131. Similar spellings are fairly common in U, e.g. (*for ǽ*) *bed* I 40, *leg* II 114; (for *ǣ*) *clenum* II 212, *grega* II 129, *sede* II 83, *þer* I 25.[2] *e* for *ǣ* also occurs in O in *geselig* III 370, and in G and O in *het* III 31. In A the spelling *æ* for *ĕ* (never *ē*) is quite common, e.g. *cwæðende* I 83, III 53, *læcgan* II 146, *swæfne* III 56, *wæras* II 37.[3] *æ* for *ě* also occurs occasionally in U, e.g. (for *ě*) *færingan* (for *ferigan*) II 145, *gewænde* II 30; (for *ē*) *bræmum* II 111, *næxtan* II 55; and once in O (for *ě*) *ændebyrdnesse* III 68. These spellings are probably better regarded as due to the late date of the MSS, than as dialectal features.[4]

[1] MS B, which attempts a systematic translation of the text into ME of the end of the twelfth century, is not considered here. The language of this MS, as it occurs in another homily in the collection (also probably a translation from OE), is described by A. S. Napier, *History of the Holy Rood-Tree* (E.E.T.S., O.S. 103) (1894).

[2] Cp also II 85, textual notes.

[3] See also I 230; II 82, 89, 100, 106, 145, 215; III 75, 76, 211, 282, 318, 335 and notes. Occasionally also in unstressed syllables, e.g. *gangænde* A I 182; *-ceastær* U I 113, *ilæs* U II 100; *rodæ* U I 27. In A *æ* has occasionally been altered to *e* by partial erasure: see textual notes on I 143, 144, 151, 153; III 11, 282, 303.

[4] MS A belonged in the thirteenth century, and probably earlier, to the Abbey of Bury St Edmunds (see RES NS ix (1958) 160 and fn. 2). If these spellings are regarded as the result of the south-eastern raising of *ǣ* to *ē* they might suggest that it was written there. On orthographic confusion of *e* and *æ* in LOE MSS, see Schlemilch, *Beiträge zur Sprache und Orthographie Spätaltengl. Sprachdenkmäler der Übergangszeit 1000–1150* (Halle, 1914) 5 f, 18 ff.

There is considerable variation, both within, and between, the various MSS, in the spelling of many words containing EWS *ĭ*, *ў̆*, *ĭe*.[1] There are a number of words in which *i* and *y* are about equally frequent, so that it is impossible to estimate the direction of scribal interference (if any).[2] Occasional *y*-spellings of words which are usually spelt in these MSS with *i*, occur in all the MSS, but are particularly frequent in A.[3] Occasional *i*-spellings of words usually spelt with *y* seem especially characteristic of O.[4]

Between the initial palatal consonants *g* and *sc* and a following back vowel, *e* is usually written, but there are occasional forms without *e* in A and O, e.g. *scamelum* A III 360, *sco* AO III 105, A III 107, *scof* A I 216, *scolde* O III 216, 256. Before *u*, however, palatal *g* is spelt *i*, *I*, and there is no diphthonging of the vowel, e.g. *iugoðe*, *Iung(e)*. Between medial palatal consonants and a back vowel, *e* is not usually written, except in the word *bisceop*.[5]

EWS *ĕo* preceded by *w* is represented by *u*, e.g. (followed by *r* + consonant) *swurd(bora)*, *wurðan*, *wurpan*, etc (but not *weorc*); (followed by consonant + back vowel) *swura*, *swustor*, *swutol* and its derivatives.[6] The very late retraction of *y* in the group *wyr* + consonant is reflected in *wurðe* UV II 210 (beside usual *wyrðe*, *wyrcan*, *andwyrdan*, etc).

Palatal *g* disappears after *i*, *e* and *æ*, with compensatory lengthening of the vowel, in, e.g., *lið* (3 sg.pres.ind. of *licgan*), *ledon*, *geled* (pret.pl. and p.pt. of *lecgan*), *sæde*, *-on*,

---

[1] Words consistently spelt with *i* or *y* are not dealt with here.

[2] E.g. (with EWS *ĭ*) *swilce/swylce*, *þider/þyder*, *þisne/þysne* (acc.sg.m.), *þis(se)re/þys(se)re* (gen. and dat.sg.f.), *þisum/þysum* (dat.sg.m. and neut., and dat.pl.), *þrim/þrym* (dat.pl.); (with EWS *ĭe*) *git/gyt*.

[3] E.g. *blyðe*, *hlyde*, *lyfigende*, *mycel*, *nys*, *scyp*, *scryne*, *smyðe*, *swyðe*, *Swyðun*, *syðian*, *þrydda*, *þrywa*, *Wynceaster*, *-wylles*: all these words have EWS *ĭ*.

[4] E.g. (with EWS *ĭ*) *bedrida*, *niste*, *simle*; (with EWS *ў̆*, *ĭe*) *dislican*, *gehiran*, *gelifan*, *scippend*, *gesine*, *sinfullan*, *ðrimwealdendum*. *Siððan* is very rare outside of AU.

[5] The spelling *biscop* is very rare, e.g. A I 58, V I 142.

[6] But *swutol* and *swustor* may derive from EWS forms with·*u*.

gesæd (pret. and p.pt. of *secgan*). As a result *i* is occasionally spelt *ig*, e.g. in the prefix *bi-*. Present forms of consonantal (weak) verbs of class 2 are spelt with *ig* or *i*: in A *ig* is usual when a front vowel follows (including the pres.pt. and infl.inf.), but is not found before a following back vowel; U, however, has a number of forms like *efesigan* II 159, *æteowigan* II 194.[1]

Palatal *g* after *r* is regularly syllabic before a consonant or back vowel, but not before a front vowel, e.g. *bebyrigdon* beside *bebyrged*, *wyri(g)an* beside *awyrgede*.

The spelling *cg* for non-palatal *g* after *n* in words like *cyning*, *þing*, etc, which is common in A, is not found in the other MSS.

Sporadic forms indicating voicing of initial *hr* occur in all the MSS, e.g. *rofes* AV I 189 (*hrofes* U); (-)*raðe* A III 332 (-*hraðe* O, -*raðe* G, but *h* erased), U I 57 (*hraþe* A);[2] and the inverted spelling *ahrærde* A I 71 (*arærde* U).[3]

Doubling of an etymologically single consonant before a liquid occurs in *micclum*, *micclan* (oblique forms of *micel*) regularly in all MSS, except *miclan* U II 209; cp also *gesicclod* A I 170 (*gesiclod* U), *riccra* U I 48 (*ricra* A), *hlæddre* A II 170 (*hlædre* U), AU II 176. In U double consonants are often simplified medially between vowels, e.g. *libe* II 70, *gemete* II 81, *syþan* II 92. Outside of U, this occurs only in O in the word *lateow* III 132, 171, etc, and, in other MSS, in unstressed syllables, e.g. inflected forms of *fæsten*, -*ræden*, etc. Doubling of single consonants between vowels is very rare, e.g. *geuntrummod* U I 203, *cucenne* AU II 61, *beswicenne* O III 365. There is considerable fluctuation in the spelling of monosyllables like *man(n)*, *ful(l)* *feol(l)*, etc.

The weakening of unstressed syllables (QW § 13) is reflected in inflectional syllables in these MSS[4] in,

---

[1] Cp also *adlian* (for *adligan*) A III 104.

[2] These forms probably belong here, although there is another word *raðe* with the same meaning, but etymologically distinct.

[3] Cp also I 174n.

[4] All the relevant examples in A are pointed out in the notes: many of them have been 'corrected' by the reviser.

(1) the frequent replacement of the back vowels *u* and *o* by *a* in, e.g., nom./acc.pl. of nouns of the neuter general (strong) declension (QW § 198), and pret.pl. of verbs;[1]

(2) a tendency to replace *a* in final syllables by *e*: this applies to *a* < *u,o* (see (1) above), as well as to original *a* in, e.g., nom.sg.m. of the definite (weak) declension of adjectives, nom./acc.pl. of nouns of the feminine general (strong) declension, gen.pl. of nouns and adjectives, and the infinitive;

(3) the occasional replacement of *-um* by *-an*, *-on* in dat.sg.m./neut. of the indefinite (strong) declension of adjectives,[2] and dat.pl. of nouns;[3]

(4) in a number of inverted spellings resulting from these changes,

    (i) *o* for *a* in, e.g., the infinitive;

    (ii) *a* for *e* in, e.g., nom.sg.f. and neut. of the definite (weak) declension of adjectives, oblique cases sg. of nouns of the feminine general (strong) declension, dat.sg. of nouns of the masculine and neuter general (strong) declensions, nom./acc.pl. of the indefinite (strong) declension of adjectives,[4] and pres.subj.pl. of verbs;[5]

---

[1] The ending *-on* (*-an*) is formally identical with the old ind., *-en* (see under (2) above) with the old subj., inflection, but their occurrence is not related to the old distinction between ind. and subj.; on the inflection of the pres.subj. see p. 11, fn. 1.

[2] In the expression *to soðan* 'truly', the ending is always *-an*, except *to soðum* A III 244.

[3] The reviser may have corrected a similar spelling at I 49 (cp textual notes).

[4] *manega* and *feawa* are the normal forms of the nom./acc.pl. of these words (possibly by analogy with *fela*). Other adjectives usually have *-e* for all genders: the special forms for the fem. and neut. are not preserved. The same is true of the special form of the nom.sg.fem. of short-stemmed adjectives and adjectives in *-e*, *-ig*, etc: the nom. sg.fem. of these adjectives is the same as the masc. and neut.

[5] The reviser of MS A is probably correcting such forms where inflectional *e* in his hand stands on erasure, e.g. I 84. On other occasions he corrects in his usual way (by underdotting and writing the correct form above), e.g. I 218; and once (I 45) by erasing the front of *a* and adding a bow to the back stroke to make *e*.

a- is very common in the nom./acc.pl. *leoda* (A 6x, U 4x; the regu-

(iii) *o* for *e* in, e.g., p.pt. of vocalic (strong) verbs, and pres.subj.pl. of all verbs;[1]

(iv) *-um* for *-an* in dat.sg.m./neut. of the definite (weak) declenion of adjectives.[2]

The medial vowel of inflected forms of the p.pt. of consonantal (weak) verbs is as a rule not syncopated: the scribe of MS A seems to be responsible for the introduction of a number of syncopated forms, e.g. *gehælde* I 26, III 265, *gebigdum* III 85. The same is possibly true of a number of other syncopated forms, e.g. *þysre* (gen./dat.sg.f.) III 367 (*þissere* GO), III 6;[3] *sawlleas* III 248 (*sawol-* O); *ægðrum* III 361 (*ægðerum* G); *orhlice* II 194 (*orgellican* U); *efsian* II 159 (*efesigan* U).

IV. AUTHOR

Ælfric, so far as the surviving documents allow us to judge, was by far the most prolific, and by far the most popular, of the Anglo-Saxon homilists. There are extant some hundred and sixty homilies which are known to be by him, or which have been attributed to him on stylistic or other grounds: most of them are contained in three

---

lar form *leode* occurs in A 7x, in U 9x), probably by analogy with f. nouns of the general declension (in particular, perhaps, *þeod*): the word represents an uncommon declensional pattern in OE (m. *i*-stems).

[1] The ending of the pres.subj.pl. is usually *-on*, less often *-an* (see (4ii) above); the old ending *-en* seems not to occur (cp p. 10, fn. 1).

[2] The occurrence of these inverted spellings seems to some extent to be determined by the possibility of morphological confusion, e.g. the infinitive in *-on* is identical with pres.subj.pl. in *-on* (the usual form in these MSS); the p.pt. of vocalic verbs in *-on* is identical with the pret.pl.; dat.sg.m./neut. of the def. declension of adjectives in *-um* is identical with the corresponding case of the indef. declension. Attraction to the form of the inflection of a neighbouring word is possible in a number of instances, e.g. II 121, 167.

[3] Unsyncopated forms of the gen./dat.sg.f. and gen.pl. occur in other homilies in A; they seem in fact to be slightly commoner than the syncopated forms.

courses of sermons for holy days and saints' days throughout the year. These are the collection from which the homilies in the present volume are taken—the *Lives of Saints*[1]—and the two series of *Catholic Homilies*.[2] The *Catholic Homilies* in all likelihood first appeared in 991–2,[3] and the *Lives of Saints* probably followed soon after:[4] they were certainly complete by 1002, the year in which the death of Æthelweard, to whom the preface is addressed, is believed to have occurred.[5]

The two series of *Catholic Homilies* contain, as Ælfric himself says, not only expositions of the gospels, but also passions and lives of saints whose festivals were observed

[1] See above, p. 1, fn. 2. Four of the 37 homilies printed by Skeat from MS A are not by Ælfric (nos. XXIII, XXIIIB, XXX, XXXIII).

[2] Ed. B. Thorpe, *The Homilies of the Anglo-Saxon Church*, 2 vols. 1844–6. In 'The chronology of Ælfric's works' (*The Anglo-Saxons, Studies presented to Bruce Dickins*, ed. Peter Clemoes (1959) 212–47), P. A. M. Clemoes lists all the pieces which he regards as Ælfric's: the three series mentioned above in their earliest extant form account for 119 of the 161 liturgical homilies and non-liturgical narrative pieces in the list. A large proportion of the remainder Clemoes believes to have been written by Ælfric for revised issues of the *Catholic Homilies*, two of which are now only fragmentarily extant; a third, a revised issue of the first series only, is preserved in MS CCCC 188 (Ker, no. 43; see also Sisam, *Studies*, 175–8). Clemoes includes among the non-liturgical narratives a number of homiletic paraphrases of books of the Old Testament, three of which (of parts of *Genesis*, *Numbers* and *Joshua*) were incorporated in the OE *Hexateuch* by the compiler of that work (cp also p. 224 and fn. 3, pp. 240 f and p. 241, fn. 1).

[3] On the dating of this and other works, see Sisam, *Studies*, 148–98, 298–301, and Clemoes, *op.cit.*

[4] Henel argues that, since they are not dedicated to Sigeric, archbishop of Canterbury, as are CH, they did not appear until after Sigeric's death, which occurred in 995 (*Ælfric's De Temporibus Anni* (E.E.T.S., O.S. 213) (1942) xlix, fn. 3; cp *Anglia* vi (1883) 426, fn. 1).

[5] Ealdorman of Wessex beyond Selwood, and himself author of a Latin Chronicle. The date of his death is not certain: see P. A. M. Clemoes, *op. cit.*, 243, fn. 1. A number of Ælfric's works were undertaken at his request, e.g. the translations of *Genesis* 'to Isaac', and of *Joshua*; cp also CH I p. 8, ll. 16 ff (on which see Sisam, *Studies*, 161 ff).

by the laity.[1] They were arranged, he says, in two books 'because he thought it would be less tedious to listen to, if the one book were read in the course of one year, and the other in the course of the next'.[2] In the third series of homilies, the *Lives of Saints* (the title given them by their first editor), he included 'as well the passions and lives of those saints whom the monks, but not the laity, honour in their services'.[3] The series was not, as has occasionally been suggested, intended for monastic reading, nor was it to consist exclusively of lives of saints whose festivals were observed only in the monasteries: in fact, eleven of the homilies (a third of the total) do not fall into this category—including six which are not for saints' days.

Ælfric was also the author of a number of grammatical works: a grammar of Latin, the first in a modern vernacular, a Latin glossary,[4] and the *Colloquy*, a model of a classroom dialogue in Latin.[5] Ælfric was a common name among the Anglo-Saxons and was borne by several men of note about the year 1000.[6] To distinguish Ælfric the writer from his various contemporaries of the same name, Anglo-Saxon scholars of the seventeenth and eighteenth centuries often refer to him as 'the Grammarian', *Ælfricus Grammaticus*, and the designation is by no means inappropriate. For, to judge from the number of manuscript copies in which the *Grammar* survives—which far exceeds that of any other work of comparable length by Ælfric, or any other vernacular writer of the Anglo-Saxon period[7]—it was easily the

[1] CH I Latin Preface ll. 18–20; CH II English Preface ll. 10–13.
[2] CH II English Preface ll. 7–9; CH I Latin Preface ll. 28–31.
[3] LS Preface ll. 8 f.
[4] Ed. J. Zupitza, *Ælfrics Grammatik und Glossar* (1880).
[5] Ed. G. N. Garmondsway, *Ælfric's Colloquy* (1938).
[6] E.g. Ælfric, archbishop of Canterbury 995–1005, Ælfric, archbishop of York 1023–1051, with both of whom attempts were in the past made to identify the writer; see also D. Whitelock, 'Two Notes on Ælfric and Wulfstan', MLR xxxviii (1943) 122–6.
[7] There are fifteen MSS copies of the Grammar extant, though not all of them are complete; five of them are of post-Conquest date, the latest being of the beginning of the thirteenth century. Individual homilies by Ælfric are preserved in an equal, or slightly larger,

most popular of his works in the Middle Ages, and the one with which his name would then have been first associated.

Of Ælfric's remaining non-homiletic works, the most important is one which, in its earliest form, occurs among a number of pieces appended to the second series of *Catholic Homilies*, where it is entitled *Epistola de Canonibus*.[1] It consists of a letter written by Ælfric for Wulfsige, bishop of Sherborne from 992 to 1002, and addressed as from him to his clergy, instructing them in their duties and in the mode of life they should lead. This work Ælfric subsequently rewrote, with alterations and additions, as two letters for Wulfstan, archbishop of York, the homilist and statesman. His first version of the two letters for Wulfstan was in Latin, but he later translated them, very freely and again with considerable additions, into English.[2] In their final form they constitute a sort of compendium for priests of canonical, liturgical and other matters.[3] Another of the pieces appended to the second series of *Catholic Homilies*, a treatise on astronomy and chronology, *De Temporibus Anni*,[4] was also intended for the clergy, to enable them to understand the complicated calculations by which the date of Easter was ascertained.

In the Latin Preface to the first series of *Catholic Homilies*, Ælfric describes himself as *alumnus Adelwoldi*, 'pupil of Æthelwold'. Æthelwold, one of the three great English monastic reformers of the tenth century, was bishop of

---

number of copies (the homilies for Monday (16 copies), and Tuesday (18 copies), in Rogationtide, for Whitsunday (17 copies), and for Easterday (15 copies) in the first series of *Catholic Homilies*).

[1] Ed. B. Fehr, *Die Hirtenbriefe Ælfrics* (Bibliothek der angelsächsischen Prosa ix) (1914).

[2] Latin and English versions edited by Fehr, *op.cit.*

[3] A similar work on the monastic life, an abridgement of the *Regularis Concordia*, made by Ælfric for his monks at Eynsham, is edited by Mary Bateson as Appendix vii of *Compotus Rolls of the Obedientiaries of St Swithun's Priory, Winchester* (ed. G. W. Kitchin, Hampshire Record Society, 1892).

[4] Ed. H. Henel (E.E.T.S., O.S. 213) (1942); the work is very largely translated from Bede.

Winchester from 963 until his death in 984. Ælfric refers with evident pride on several occasions elsewhere in his writings,[1] to his education under Æthelwold at Winchester, and eventually wrote, in Latin, a biography of his master.[2] In the English Preface to the first series of *Catholic Homilies*, Ælfric says he was sent by Ælfheah, Æthelwold's successor as bishop of Winchester,[3] to the monastery of Cernel,[4] which had been founded in 987 by Æthelmær, son of the ealdorman Æthelweard.[5] There also he speaks of himself as *munuc and mæssepreost*, so that he must by this time have been at least thirty, the minimum age for ordination to the priesthood.[6] In 1005 Æthelmær founded another monastery at Eynsham near Oxford, and Ælfric became its first abbot. The date of his death is not known.[7]

V. SOURCES

All Ælfric's vernacular works were undertaken with one aim in view: to enable his countrymen to enjoy the spiritual benefits to be derived from a knowledge of the Latin literature of the church, by making available to them in their own language some of the literature itself, and the means of learning for themselves the language in which it was written.

[1] See Skeat, vol. ii, pp. xli f.

[2] Ed. J. Stevenson (R.S. 2 (ii), 1858); *Cat. Cod. Hag. Lat. BN Paris* (1890) Appendix; there is a translation in *English Historical Documents c. 500–1042* (ed. Dorothy Whitelock, 1955) 831–9.

[3] St Alphege, bishop of Winchester 984–1005, afterwards archbishop of Canterbury; martyred by the Danes 1012.

[4] Now Cerne Abbas, Dorset.

[5] On Æthelweard, see above, p. 12, fn. 5. Æthelmær succeeded his father as ealdorman of Wessex beyond Selwood. It was in response to his, as well as his father's, requests for such writings, that Ælfric compiled the *Lives of Saints* (LS Preface ll. 38 ff). On Æthelmær, see A. J. Robertson, *Anglo-Saxon Charters* (1939) 386 f.

[6] The preface was probably written 990–1, certainly not later than 995.

[7] It is usually said to be probably after 1012, possibly after 1020, on the strength of his supposed attestation of charters in those years; but see D. Whitelock, MLR xxxviii (1943) 122–4.

Each of his works has its place in this 'plan for education in
the vernacular comparable to Alfred's plan a century
earlier, but more systematic and concentrated on the
advancement of religion'.[1] In the prefaces to his various
works he states his purpose in writing them:

> Rash, or rather, presumptuous, though it is to have done so,
> nevertheless I have translated this volume out of Latin books
> (that is to say holy scriptures) into the language to which we are
> accustomed, for the edification of the unlearned who know only
> this language, either through reading it, or hearing it read.[2]

> This volume also I have translated from Latin into the
> language in ordinary use in England, desiring to benefit others,
> by strengthening them in faith through reading this narrative,
> who are willing to take the trouble either to read this work, or to
> listen to it read.[3]

There were many things which he felt it was impossible, or
undesirable, to communicate to lay audiences in this way;[4]
and he seems to have had continual misgivings about the
whole undertaking: 'he was uneasy about the whole policy
of Englishing, and from the outset we find him closing the
ways against more'.[5] But it was the duty of the learned to
teach, as he himself repeatedly urged, not only for the
benefit of the souls of those whom they taught, but of their
own as well.[6]

His first concern was for the soundness of his doctrine,
'guarding most carefully against misleading errors, lest I be
found seduced by any heresy, or darkened by falsehood';[7]
and it was, he says, because he had 'seen and heard much

[1] Sisam, *Studies*, 301.

[2] CH I Latin Preface ll. 3–7.

[3] LS Preface ll. 1–4; cp also ll. 14–17, 70 f; Preface to the *Grammar*, etc.

[4] See, e.g., CH I Latin Preface ll. 24 ff; LS Preface ll. 9 ff; Preface
to *Genesis* ll. 41 ff.

[5] Sisam, *Studies*, 171, fn. 1; see, e.g., LS Preface ll. 29 ff; Preface to
Genesis ll. 113 ff.

[6] CH I English Preface p. 6, ll. 20 ff; Preface to *Grammar*, p. 2,
ll. 19 ff; HB I 63 f, II 3, III 80–5, etc.

[7] CH I Latin Preface ll. 12 ff.

false doctrine in many English books, which unlearned men in their innocence accounted great wisdom', that he wrote the first book of *Catholic Homilies*.[1] He pleads continually with the scribes to copy his work accurately, and not to mix up other people's work with his own—not through any pride of authorship, but to ensure that his efforts to make his work reliable should not be wasted:

Now I beg and beseech, in God's name, that if anyone wishes to copy this book, that he correct it assiduously by the exemplar, lest I be made blameworthy by faulty copyists. He does great evil who produces a faulty copy, unless he corrects it: it is as if he should turn true doctrine into false error. And so he must correct what he has made corrupt, if he wishes to be guiltless at God's judgement.[2]

Ælfric lays no claim to originality:

I say nothing new in this book, for it has stood written in Latin books for a long time, though the unlearned did not know of it; nor will I falsely pretend to do so, for fathers strong in faith, and holy teachers wrote it in Latin for a lasting memorial, and for the edification of future generations.[3]

He usually refers to his works as translations—though they would certainly not be regarded as such today.[4] It was not his intention, as he himself says, to produce a literal translation:

I have not been able in this translation always to translate word for word, but I have taken great pains to render sense for sense,[5] as I found it in holy writings, in such clear and simple

---

[1] CH I English Preface ll. 6 ff.

[2] CH I English Preface p. 8, ll. 9 ff; cp CH II English Preface ll. 15 ff, Oratio p. 594, ll. 7 ff; LS Preface ll. 74 ff; Preface to *Genesis* ll. 117 ff; Preface to *Grammar* p. 3, ll. 20 ff.

[3] LS Preface ll. 46–52.

[4] Cp Sisam, *Studies*, 299, fn. 2: ' "Adapt" is nearer than "translate" to Ælfric's sense of *transferre* and *awendan*'. See also A. E. Nichols, '*Awendan*: A Note on Ælfric's Vocabulary', JEGP lxiii (1964) 7–13, and cp H. J. Chaytor, *From Script to Print* (Cambridge 1950) 89, fn. 1.

[5] For Latin and OE parallels, see Max Förster, *Ueber die Quellen von Ælfrics Hom. Cath.* (Diss. Berlin 1892) 8, fn.; Ælfric himself also uses the phrase at CH I Latin Preface ll. 11 f, and HB II 1.

language as may profit the hearers. Furthermore it should be understood that I have shortened the longer narratives, as regards the language, but not the sense, in case the fastidious should be bored by their being told in our language at as great length as in Latin—and brevity does not always mar discourse, but often makes it more beautiful.[1]

But this gives an inadequate—even misleading—impression of the extent of the liberties he takes with his originals. In fact, as well as paraphrasing and summarizing freely, he makes quite extensive omissions and changes in the arrangement of the material; occasionally he makes additions of his own, or combines material from different sources.[2] The homilies in this volume are completely typical in these respects of Ælfric's treatment of his sources.

Almost the whole of the homily on St Oswald is derived from Bede's *Historia Ecclesiastica Gentis Anglorum*.[3] In it Ælfric has assembled and rearranged almost all the information concerning Oswald given by Bede,[4] to form an account, on the conventional pattern, of the life, passion, and miracles of the saint. Ælfric was indebted to Bede for material for his homilies more often than to any other author except Gregory the Great; in particular, the *Historia Ecclesiastica* was the source of two others of the *Lives of Saints*, those of St Alban and St Æthelthryth.

The homily on St Edmund is based on the *Passio Sancti Eadmundi* of Abbo of Fleury.[5] In the brief preface to his

[1] LS Preface ll. 22–9; Ælfric's remarks on literal translation in the preface to *Genesis* (ll. 95–101) should be compared.

[2] See also D. Bethurum, 'The form of Ælfric's Lives of the Saints', SP xxix (1932) 519–28.

[3] Ed. C. Plummer (1896, 1946). There is a convenient translation by Leo Sherley-Price (Penguin Books, 1955). Ælfric mentions Bede's 'book' at l. 224 (cp also l. 27). Although it is clear from CH II pp. 116 f that Ælfric knew of the OE version of Bede's HE, there is no reason to believe that he made use of it in writing the homily on St Oswald; see also I 152n.

[4] Chiefly in the first thirteen chapters of Book iii: details of the relationship of the homilies to their sources are given in the commentary.

[5] Ed. Thomas Arnold, *Memorials of St Edmund's Abbey* (R.S. 96)

homily, Ælfric states that it is a translation of this work, and relates how Abbo, monk and later abbot of Fleury, while visiting Dunstan, archbishop of Canterbury, three years before Dunstan's death, had learnt the story of St Edmund from the archbishop himself, who, when a young man, had heard Edmund's own sword-bearer, then a very old man, tell it to King Athelstan. Dunstan, the leader of the English Benedictine revival of the tenth century, was born about 909 of noble parents, and as a young man was attached to the court of Athelstan, who became king in 924, fifty-five years after Edmund's death.[1] Dunstan died in 988, so that Abbo's visit to England belongs to the years 985–7. Abbo, one of the most learned men in Europe in his day, had been invited to England by Oswald, bishop of Worcester and archbishop of York, to teach at the monastery which Oswald had founded at Ramsey in Huntingdonshire. In the prefatory letter addressed to Dunstan, Abbo says that it was at the earnest entreaty of the monks of Ramsey that he undertook to write the book. As Ælfric relates, Abbo became abbot of Fleury soon after his return from England; he died in 1004.[2]

Ælfric's account of the miracles of St Swithin is, in the main, a very free translation and abridgement of the *Libellus de Miraculis S. Suithuni Episcopi* of Landferth.[3] Ælfric

---

(1890) i 3 ff, from the Bodleian MS Fell 4, with collations from three of the numerous other MSS (for a list of these, see Hardy, *Descriptive Catalogue* (R.S. 26) i 526): references in the commentary to Abbo are to this edition. See also Grant Loomis, 'The Growth of the St Edmund Legend', HSN xiv (1932) 83–113, which contains a summary of Abbo's work, and relates it to earlier and subsequent accounts of St Edmund.

[1] For Dunstan see esp. J. Armitage Robinson, *The Times of Saint Dunstan* (1923) ch. IV.

[2] On Abbo see T. Arnold, *op.cit.*, xxii f, and Rose Graham, *English Ecclesiastical Studies* (1929) 105 f.

[3] The text in *Acta SS. Iul.* (1867) i 294–9 is from the Vatican MS Reginae Sueciae 566 (formerly 769), which is imperfect, containing only chapters IV to XXX (ii 1–46). The prefatory material (i 1–4) and chapters I–III (i 5–24), XXXI–XXXVIII (ii 47–54), were

relates, often in a very condensed form, only 17 of the 38 miracles in Landferth's book, which he mentions (though not as his source) in ll. 334 f. The book is Landferth's only known work, and nothing is known about him beyond what can be deduced from it—which is very little.[1] From the prefatory letter it appears that he wrote his book at the request of the monks of Winchester cathedral, to whom the letter is addressed. From his own words again (c. III (i 24)), we learn that he was writing only ten years after the translation in 971 of St Swithin's remains into the cathedral from the humble grave outside, where they had lain since his death in 862.

Ælfric seems also to have had access to another, shorter, Latin account of St Swithin, referred to here as the *Epitome*.[2] So far as it goes, this work is very similar to Land-

---

printed from Rouen MS U. 107 by E. P. Sauvage in *Analecta Bollandiana* iv (1885) 367–410. The version preserved in BM MSS Royal 15 C. vii (described by John Earle, *Gloucester Fragments* (1861) 60–6), and Cotton Nero E I, differs slightly from that printed by the Bollandists (in particular in the order of the chapters, in the wording of some of the rubrics, and in the addition of an extra chapter). The printed texts are divided by the editors into two series of paragraphs, numbered 1 to 24, and 1 to 54: references to Landferth here and in the commentary are given according to the chapter numbers of the Rouen MS, followed in brackets by these editorial paragraph numbers.

Landferth's book also formed the basis of the Latin *Narratio Metrica de Sancto Swithuno* by Ælfric's contemporary, Wulfstan, cantor of Winchester (ed. A. Campbell, Turici, 1950).

[1] Sauvage pointed out (p. 369) that the tone of the dedicatory epistle makes it unlikely that he was, as is often stated, a monk of Winchester himself. Ælfric calls him (l. 334) *se ofersæwisca*, 'the foreigner': I do not think it has been noticed before that in the passage corresponding to Sauvage ii 47 l. 6, the Royal MS has *sacerdos quidam nomine Lantfredus*. His name may be English, but more probably represents a naturalization of the German name Landfrid (see T. Forssner, *Continental-Germanic Personal Names in England* (1916) 173; O. von Feilitzen, *Pre-Conquest Personal Names of Domesday Book* (1937) 308 f).

[2] Printed in *Acta SS* (as above) 292–3 from the Paris MS BN Lat. 5362 (which also contains the only extant copy of Ælfric's life of St Æthelwold).

ferth's, with which it is obviously connected in some way, though whether it is actually an abridgement or an earlier draft of his book it would be hard to say. The fact that Ælfric's summary of Landferth is sometimes very close to the brief statements of the same material in this document, may be no more than a coincidence; but there are some details in both it and Ælfric which are not in Landferth.[1]

VI. STYLE

Most of Ælfric's *Lives of Saints* (including the three homilies printed here[2]), and many others of his homilies, are written in a kind of rhythmical prose, similar in form to the alliterative verse of, for example, *Beowulf*, but more freely constructed. The manuscripts of these homilies, like all Old English manuscripts—including those of texts in verse—are written continuously. The homilies, however, are found to consist of an unbroken series of pairs of short phrases, usually linked together by alliteration; the phrases are all of about equal length, and each as a rule contains two stressed syllables:

On Éadgares dágum   ðæs ǽðelan cýnincges,

þa ða se crístendom   wæs wél ðéonde

þurh Gód on Ángelcynne   under ðam ýlcan cýnincge,

þa geswútelode Gód   þone sánct Swýðun

mid mánegum wúndrum,   þæt he mǽre ís.[3]

---

[1] See notes on ll. 1–11, 34–5, 186–218, 200–1; see also G. H. Gerould, 'Ælfric's Legend of St Swithin', *Anglia* xxxii (1909) 346–57.

[2] Except the preface to *St Edmund* (ll. 1–13), which is in ordinary prose.

[3] III 1–4. In Skeat's edition the homilies in this style are printed as verse; see his remarks vol. i, pp. vi f, and vol. ii, pp. l–liii. He suggests (vol. i, p. vii, vol. ii, p. li), that the punctuation of MS A is metrical, but this appears not to be the case. The punctuation of all the MSS is partly syntactical, partly elocutionary, and appears in all essential features to be identical with that found in MSS of the CH,

The range of patterns of alliteration,[1] and of stressed and unstressed syllables, is much more diverse than in the verse, and the number of unstressed syllables is on average larger, particularly the number of those preceding the first stress. Nevertheless a general resemblance is clear. Apart however from the rhythm and alliteration, Ælfric's writing in this style shows no trace of the other stylistic features of Old English verse, in particular its characteristic diction and use of variation. Furthermore, since both rhythm and alliteration are so freely variable (alliteration sometimes disappears altogether), they have little effect on syntax or vocabulary.[2] Apart in fact from the rhythm and alliteration, Ælfric's writing in this style is hardly to be distinguished from his ordinary prose. Ælfric was a didactic writer: his purpose in writing was to instruct and edify. His use of the rhythmical style was perhaps intended to further these ends by increasing the appeal and effectiveness of his writing, but it was

---

described by C. G. Harlow, 'Punctuation in some MSS of Ælfric', RES NS x (1959) 1–19. Of course, since the rhythmical units are also syntactical units, and so potentially units of delivery, the punctuation usually occurs at the end of the 'verse' or 'half-verse'. Single 'half-verses' are quite often set off by punctuation; more often, however, the punctuation-unit consists of two, sometimes more (up to six), 'half-verses'. The MSS differ to some extent in the actual marks of punctuation used, but there is close agreement on the density of the punctuation, and fairly close agreement on the placing of it, between MSS G, U, and A (in its original state: in *St Oswald* and *St Swithin* a number of marks of punctuation have been erased); MS B is more lightly punctuated than the others; in MSS O and V the punctuation is not always legible owing to the damage these MSS have suffered. In the present edition the punctuation (but not the sentence division) is editorial: the punctuation of MS A (in its revised state) is reproduced, not always accurately, in Skeat's edition; that of MS G can be seen in the facsimile. See also B. Assmann, *Anglia* ix (1886) 42, and *Anglia* x (1888) 83.

[1] See A. Brandeis, 'Die Alliteration in Aelfric's metrischen Homilien', *Jahres-Bericht der K. K. Staats-Realschule im VII Bezirke in Wien 1896–7*, 3–32.

[2] For some of the syntactical differences see C. R. Barrett, *Studies in the Word-Order of Ælfric's Catholic Homilies and Lives of the Saints* (1953).

plainly subordinate to the clear and simple exposition of his matter, which remained his chief stylistic concern.[1] The rhythmical style occurs in none of the homilies in his first series of *Catholic Homilies*, and in only a few of the second, which seems to indicate that he adopted it towards the end of the composition of that work. Once having adopted it, however, he appears to have used it in all his subsequent homiletic writing.[2] It is clearly essentially an oral style, which depends for its effect on being heard. The *Lives of Saints* were probably meant for private use, not, like the *Catholic Homilies*, to be preached in church,[3] and Ælfric refers to both readers and hearers in the Latin Preface,[4] but, in an age when 'a man read aloud or at least moved his lips even in reading to himself',[5] the distinction was obviously of less significance in this context than it would be now.

It seems probable that this style is peculiar to Ælfric: at least there seems to be no Old English writing extant in the style which on other grounds it would be impossible to attribute to him.[6] However there were current from the second half of the tenth century, and perhaps earlier, in addition to the plain prose style and the strict verse style, a number of intermediate styles, broadly similar to this of Ælfric's. The best known of these is the style of Archbishop

[1] See the passage from LS Preface quoted above pp. 17 f; and cp CH I Latin Preface ll. 7 ff, and CH II Latin Preface ll. 8–14. Ælfric nowhere mentions his use of rhythm and alliteration—unless this is what he means by the expression *on ure wisan*, which he uses twice in the *Treatise on the Old Testament* (ed. Crawford, ll. 770, 777) with reference to his translations of *Esther* and *Judith* (cp CH II p. 520, l. 10 *on leoðwison*, 'in verse').

[2] See P. A. M. Clemoes, *op. cit.*, 223, fn. 3.

[3] See Clemoes, *op. cit.*, 220.

[4] ll. 4, 15, 17, 25; cp also CH I Latin Preface l. 9.

[5] Angus McIntosh, 'Wulfstan's Prose', *Proc. Brit. Acad.* xxxv (1949) 124; see also note 24.

[6] On the Ely Charter see McIntosh, *op. cit.*, 113 and note 8; see also III 369–86n and 375–7n. On the connection between Ælfric's rhythmical style and that of later homiletic and religious prose in English, see R. W. Chambers, *The Continuity of English Prose* (1932), and D. Bethurum, 'The connection of the Katherine Group with Old English prose', JEGP xxxiv (1935) 553–64.

Wulfstan; another is exemplified in the passages of 'debased verse' which occur in the Chronicle and in some of the Vercelli homilies;[1] elsewhere in the Chronicle, in the Vercelli, Blickling and other homilies still others of these styles are to be found.[2] It seems certain that all these styles are in some way related to each other and to the strict verse, but it is impossible, for the present at least, to do more than guess at the exact nature of these relationships. Much of the Latin prose of the early Middle Ages, including some of Ælfric's own, and many of his sources, also uses rhyme, rhythm and alliteration. It is possible that this fact may have influenced Ælfric in his choice of the rhythmical style, as it may also have encouraged the development of vernacular rhythmical prose in general; but the form of Ælfric's prose seems to owe little, if anything, to that of the Latin.[3]

[1] E.g. Chronicle s.a. 975 DE, 1036 CD; Vercelli II (ed. M. Förster, *Studien zur englischen Philologie* l (1913) 74 ff); see further McIntosh, *op. cit.*, 110 f, 113 and notes 2 and 7.

[2] E.g. Chronicle s.a. 979 E, 1011 E, 1086 E, etc. (see further E. V. K. Dobbie, *Anglo-Saxon Poetic Records* VI (1942) pp. xxxii f, and xxxiii fn. 1); Vercelli IV, Blickling V, etc. Some of the material of the Vercelli and Blickling homilies, together with other material of the same kind, is to be found among the spurious homilies in Napier's *Wulfstan*, e.g. XXX, XL, XLIX. Occasional alliterating and rhythmical phrases occur in many texts, including some belonging to the ninth century and earlier, which are otherwise written in plain prose: see O. Funke, 'Studien zur alliterierenden und rhythmisierenden prosa in der älteren altenglischen homiletik', *Anglia* lxxx (1962) 9-36; D. Bethurum, 'Stylistic Features of the Old English Laws', MLR xxvii (1932) 263-79; R. Vleeskruyer, *The Life of St Chad* (1953) 19 ff.

[3] See G. H. Gerould, 'Abbot Ælfric's Rhythmic Prose', MP xxii (1925) 353-66 and D. Bethurum, 'The form of Ælfric's Lives of the Saints', SP xxix (1932) 515-33.

LIVES OF
THREE ENGLISH SAINTS

The text is based on MS A: all departures from the reading of the MS as defined above p. 1, fn. 2 are printed in square brackets, including any additions or alterations made by the reviser which have been incorporated in the text. Where readings from the damaged MSS O and V are given in the footnotes, square brackets indicate letters no longer present, or totally illegible, round brackets letters imperfectly legible (see p. 2, fn. 1). Contractions are expanded without notice: *æft* as *æfter*, 7 as *and* (conjunction and prefix), *ƀ* as *bisceop*, *cō* as *com*, *cƿ* as *cwæð*, *driht* as *drihten*, *scē* as *sancte*, *ƥ* as *þæt*, *þā* as *þam*, *poñ* as *ponne* or *pone*, *-ū* as *-um*, etc. The sentence division of MS A has been retained: departures from it are indicated in the usual way. Other punctuation, word-division, paragraphing and capitalization of proper names are editorial. Accents are not reproduced. In the textual notes the account of variants is intended to be complete, except for purely orthographic variants and variation in prefixes in B (e.g. omission of *ge-*, *a-*; *a-* for *ge-*, and vice versa, etc.) unless supported by another MS. MSS which support the reading of the text are cited, as well as those which disagree: if the sigil for any MS does not appear in support of the text, or of the variant, it is because the MS is defective at that point. The spelling is guaranteed only for the first MS cited.

I

ST OSWALD, KING AND MARTYR

Æfter ðan ðe Augustinus to Engla lande becom, wæs sum
æðele cyning, Oswold gehaten, on Norðhymbra lande,
gelyfed swyþe on God; se ferde on his iugoðe fram freondum
and magum to Scotlande on sæ, and þær sona wearð
[ge]fullod, and his geferan samod þe [him mid] siþedon.
Betwux þam wearð ofslagen Eadwine his eam, Norðhymbra
cynincg, on Crist gelyfed, fram Brytta cyninge, Cedwalla

VARIANTS: 2 *æðele*] A, final -*e* possibly by rev. on erasure; om. U.
3 *se*] A; *Se* U. *his* inserted before *freondum* in A by rev.; om. U.
5 *gefullod*] AU, in A *ge* inserted by rev. 5 *him mid*] U; *mid him* A.
6 *þam*] A; *þisum* U. 7 *cedwalla*] AU, in A altered to *ceadwalla* by rev.

---

1 f *Æfter* . . . *lande:* Augustine came to England in 597; Oswald
was king in Northumbria from 633 to 641.

3 *se ferde* . . . 5 *siþedon:* from Bede HE iii 1 (on Oswald's conver-
sion cp also iii 3). Oswald and his brothers were actually driven into
exile (see below ll. 6–8n). Scotland is used in the modern sense, as
here, from the 10th century (see Plummer II 11 f, ii 138).

5 *him mid:* in subordinate clauses of this kind, *mid* normally fol-
lows the pronoun it governs, e.g. l. 63 below, II 190 and III 290,
and I have therefore adopted the reading of U. On postpositive
prepositions generally see QW § 141.

6 *Betwux þam* . . . 8 *geciged:* from Bede HE ii 20. Edwin was
Oswald's mother's brother; he belonged to the royal family of Deira,
the southernmost of the two English kingdoms north of the Humber;
Oswald's father, Æthelfrith, belonged to the royal family of Bernicia,
the northernmost kingdom. Æthelfrith drove Edwin into exile and
ruled over both kingdoms. He was killed in 616 and Edwin in his turn
took possession of both kingdoms, driving his nephews, the sons of
Æthelfrith, into exile. Edwin was slain on October 12 632: the ex-
pansion of Northumbria at the beginning of the seventh century
inevitably led to conflict with the surviving British kingdoms in the
west; the attack on Edwin by Cedwalla, king of Gwynnedd (North
Wales), seems to have been in retaliation for an invasion of his king-
dom by Edwin in the previous year. The circumstances of Edwin's
conversion are related by Bede HE ii 9–14.

7 *Cedwalla:* for the LWS simplification of diphthongs after initial
palatals (cp textual notes), see Campbell § 312; the Welsh form of the
name is *Cadwallon.*

geciged, and twegen his æftergengan binnan twam gearum;
and se Cedwalla sloh, and to sceame tucode, þa Norðhym-
10 bran leode æfter heora hlafordes fylle, oð þæt Oswold se
eadiga his yfelnysse adwæscte. Oswold him com to and him
cenlice wiðfeaht mid lytlum werode, ac his geleafa hine
getrymde and Crist him gefylste to his feonda slege.

Oswold þa arærde ane rode sona, Gode to wurðmynte, ær
15 þan þe he to ðam gewinne come, and clypode to his geferum,
'Uton feallan to ðære rode and þone Ælmihtigan biddan þæt
he us ahredde wið þone modigan feond þe us afyllan wile:
God sylf wat geare þæt we winnað rihtlice wið þysne reðan
cyning to ahreddenne ure leode.' Hi feollon þa ealle mid
20 Oswolde on gebedum and syþþan on [æ]rne mergen eodon to

8 *geciged*] A; *gehaten* U. 9 *cedwalla*] AU, in A altered to *ceadwalla*
by rev. 10 *hlafordes*] A; *hlaforda* U. 20 *cyninge* inserted after *oswolde*
in A by rev.; om. U. 20 *ærne*] U; *oðerne* A. *mergen*] A, *r* inserted
by original scribe; *morgen* U.

8 *and twegen* . . . 13 *slege:* from Bede HE iii 1. Edwin was suc-
ceeded in Deira by his cousin Osric, and in Bernicia by his nephew
Eanfrith, Oswald's brother. The battle in which Oswald defeated
Cedwalla took place 'in the last weeks of 633' (Stenton, p. 81).
Æftergengan is nom.pl.: Ælfric sometimes uses the numerals (as also
healf, sum and *mænig*) attributively with definite expressions, where
modern English uses a partitive phrase: 'two of his successors' (cp
Schrader §§ 58, 83(3), 86).

10 *hlafordes:* i.e. Edwin's; *hlaforda,* the reading of U, may be a
copyist's improvement intended to refer to Edwin and his immediate
successors (cp preceding note), but it looks more like an error due to
the final -*a* of the preceding word.

14 *Oswold* . . . 22 *geleafan,* 24 *Seo ylce* . . . 36 *ecnysse:* from Bede
HE iii 2.

14 *Gode to wurðmynte:* 'to the glory of God'; for this construction,
which is very common (cp ll. 50, 112 below, II 98, etc, and with gen.
after *to,* II 99), see QW § 108, and *Primer* § 87(1).

20 *on ærne mergen:* the reading of U agrees better with Bede
incipiente diluculo, 'as it was beginning to grow light'. *Ærne:* the
adj. *ær* occurs only in this phrase, which is commoner in Ælfric's
writings, and in LWS generally, than the cpd. *ærmorgen* (or -*mergen*).
mergen: the mutated form (on which see SB § 237 Anm. 2) is used
in all cases, regularly by Ælfric, and frequently elsewhere, especially
in LWS; the *g* is palatal, and had probably become syllabic, since the
spellings *merigen, merien* are not uncommon.

þam gefeohte and gewunnon þær sige swa swa se Wealdend
him uðe for Oswoldes geleafan, and aledon heora fynd, þone
modigan Cedwallan mid his micclan werode, þe wende þæt
him ne mihte nan werod wiðstandan. Seo ylce rod siððan,
þe Oswold þær arærde, on wurðmynte þær stod; and wurdon 25
fela gehælde untrumra manna and eac swilce nytena þurh
ða ylcan rode, swa swa us rehte Beda. Sum man feoll on
ise, þæt his earm tobærst, and læg þa on bedde gebrocod
forðearle, oð þæt man him fette of ðære foresædan rode
sumne dæl þæs meoses þe heo mid beweaxen wæs; and se 30
adliga sona on slæpe wearð gehæled on ðære ylcan nihte
þurh Oswoldes geearnung[a]. Seo stow is gehaten Heofon-
feld on Englisc, wið þone langan weall þe þa Romaniscan
worhtan, þær þær Oswold oferwan þone wælhreowan cyn-
incg; and þær wearð siþþan aræred swiðe mære cyrce Gode 35
to wurðmynte, þe wunað a on ecnysse.

Hwæt ða Oswold ongann embe Godes willan to smeagenne
sona swa he rices geweold, and wolde gebigan his leoda to

21 *eall* inserted before *wealdend* in A by rev.; om. U. 22 *him*] A,
altered to *heom* by rev.; *him* U. *uðe*] A; *geuðe* U. 29 *man him*] A;
him man U. 30 *þæs*] A; om. U. 32 *geearnunga*] U; *geearnungum* A,
-*ū* on erasure by rev. 34 *oferwan*] A, altered to *oferwann* by rev.;
oferwann U.

22 *and aledon . . . 24 wiðstandan:* Bede HE iii 1 (p. 128).

32 *geearnunga:* acc.pl.; the original reading of A may have been
-*a* or -*e* (cp l. 160 below and III 328, and see Intro. p. 10): Ælfric does
not use the dat. after *þurh* in these homilies (see also RES NS ix
(1958) 163, fn. 2).

32 f *Heofonfeld:* the name has been connected with Hallington
(Northumberland) (earlier *Halidene* < OE *halig denu,* 'holy valley')
where, according to a tradition reported by Leland, 'Oswald won the
batelle' (see A. Mawer, *The Place-Names of Northumberland and
Durham* (1920) 99, and Plummer II 123). The chapel of St Oswald-in-
Lee, built about 1737, which is believed to occupy the site of the
church built by the monks of Hexham (ll. 35 f below, HE iii 2),
stands just north of the line of the Roman Wall about five miles
south-west of Hallington and about four miles north of Hexham.

34 *worhtan:* pret.pl., see Intro. p. 10.

37 *Hwæt ða . . . 47 willan,* 49 *Hwæt ða . . . 60 geleafan:* from Bede
HE iii 3.

geleafan and to þam lifigendan Gode: sende ða to Scot-
40 lande, þær se geleafa wæs ða, and bæd ða heafodmenn þæt
hi his benum getiþodon and him sumne lareow sendon þe
his leoda mihte to Gode geweman; and him wearð þæs
getiþod. Hi sendon þa sona þam gesæligan cyninge sumne
arwurðne bisceop, Aidan gehaten, se wæs mæres lifes man
45 on munuclicre drohtnunga and he ealle woruldcara awearp
fram his heortan, nanes þinges wilnigende butan Godes
willan. Swa hwæt swa him becom of þæs cyninges gifum,
oððe ricra manna, þæt he hraðe dælde þearfum and wædlum
mid welwillendum mode. Hwæt ða Oswold cyning his cymes
50 fægnode, and hine arwurðlice underfeng his folce to ðearfe,
þæt heora geleafa wurde awend eft to Gode fram þam
wiþersæce þe hi to [ge]wende wæron. Hit gelamp þa swa
þæt se geleaffulla cyning gerehte his witan on heora agenum
gereorde þæs bisceopes bodunge mid bliþum mode and wæs

39 sende] A; Sende U. 40 wæs ða] A; ða wæs U. 41 getiþodon] A, ge
inserted by original scribe; getiðodan U. 43 gesæligan] A; om. U. 45
drohtnunga] A, -a altered to -e by rev.; drohtnunge U. 49 welwillen-
dum] AU, in A -um on erasure (by rev.?). 50 folce] AU, in A followed
by erasure of one letter. 52 wiþersæce] AU, in A æ altered from a.
gewende] AU, in A ge added by rev., preceded by erasure of three or
four letters. 54 bodunge] AU, in A preceded by ge erased.

39 sende ða: the omission of the pronominal subject is idiomatic;
there are several other examples in these homilies, e.g. ll. 181, 216
below, II 88, 103, etc.

40 þær se geleafa wæs ða: Ælfric omits HE iii 4, in which Bede gives
an account of the conversion of the Picts by the Irish and the founda-
tion of the monastery of Iona; Aidan was a monk of Iona (cp l. 45
below, on munuclicre drohtnunga).

42 him . . . 43 getiþod: (ge)tiðian, which, when active, takes a gen.
(or rarely dat.) object of thing, and dat. of person, is used imperson-
ally when passive, the objects remaining in the gen. and dat. (cp also
LS II 401, CH I 330/30).

45 drohtnunga: dat.sg., see Intro. p. 10.

47 Swa hwæt swa . . . 49 mode: from Bede HE iii 5 (p. 135).

52 wiþersæce: after Edwin's death Northumbria largely reverted
to heathendom; see Bede HE ii 20, on the withdrawal of the Roman
mission, and iii 1, on the apostasy of Edwin's successors.

53 witan: dat.pl., see Intro. p. 10.

his wealhstod, for þan þe he wel cuþe Scyttysc and se ₅₅
bisceop Aidan ne mihte gebigan his spræce to Norðhym-
briscum gereorde swa hraþe þagit.

Se biscop þa ferde bodigende geond eall Norhymbra
lan[d] geleafan and fulluht, and þa leode gebigde to Godes
geleafan, and him wel gebysnode mid weorcum symle, and ₆₀
sylf swa leofode swa swa he lærde oðr[um]. He lufode
forhæfednysse and halige rædinge, and [i]unge men teah
georne mid lare, swa þæt ealle his geferan þe him mid eodon
sceoldon sealmas leornian oððe sume rædinge, swa hwider
swa hi ferdon þam folce bodigende. Seldon he wolde ridan, ₆₅
ac siðode on his fotum, and munuclice leofode betwux ðam
læwedum folce mid mycelre gesceadwisnysse and soþum
mægnum.

þa wearð se cynincg Oswold swiðe ælmesgeorn and
eadmod on þeawum and on eallum þingum cystig; and man ₇₀
ahrærde cyrcan on his rice geond eall, and mynsterlice
gesetnysse, mid micelre geornfulnysse. Hit gelamp on
sumne sæl þæt hi sæton ætgædere, Oswold and Aidan, on
þam halgan Easterdæge; þa bær man þam cyninge cynelice
þenunga on anum sylfrenan disce, and sona þa inn eode ₇₅

59 *land*] U; *lande* A. 61 *oðrum*] U; *oðre* A, -*e* on erasure of two
letters by rev. 62 *iunge*] U; *Iunge* A. 65 *Seldon*] A; *seldon* U.
69 *ælmesgeorn*] AU, in A one letter erased after *s*. 72 *gesetnysse*] AU,
in A -*e* altered to -*a* by rev. *mid*] A; *and mid* U. *gelamp*] A; *gelamp
ða* U. 73 *ætgædere*] A; *togædere* U.

60 *and him . . . 68 mægnum*: from Bede HE iii 5 (Ælfric omits
Bede's account at the end of this chapter of an earlier, unsuccessful
mission from Iona).
61 *oðrum*: for *læran* with dat. cp CH I 74/21 f.
67 *læwedum*: dat.sg.neut.def. (wk.), see Intro. p. 11.
69 *þa wearð . . . 70 cystig, 72 Hit gelamp . . . 91 wurðode*: from
Bede HE iii 6.
70 *and man . . . 72 geornfulnysse*: from Bede HE iii 3 (p. 132).
71 *ahrærde*: inorganic *h*, see Intro. p. 9.
72 *gesetnysse*: acc.pl., see Intro. p. 10, and cp textual notes.
75 *sylfrenan*: dat.sg.m.indef. (strong), see Intro. p. 9; an adj.
after *an* normally has the indef. declension, e.g. below l. 187, III 132,
242; cp Schrader § 43.

an þæs cyninges þegna þe his ælmyssan bewiste, and sæde
þæt fela þearfan sætan geond þa stræt, gehwanon cumene
to þæs cyninges ælmyssan. Þa sende se cyning sona þam
þearfum þone sylfrenan disc mid sand[um] mid ealle, and
80 het toceorfan þone disc and syllan þam þearfum heora
ælcum his dæl; and man dyde ða swa. Þa genam Aidanus se
æðela bisceop þæs cyninges swyþran hand mid swiðlicre
blysse and clypode mid geleafan, þus cwæðende him to, 'Ne
forrotige on brosnung[e] þ[es] gebletsode swyðr[a]l'; and
85 him eac swa geeode, swa swa Aidanus him bæd, þæt his
swiðre hand is gesundful oð þis.

Oswoldes cynerice wearð gerymed þa swyðe, swa þæt
feower þeoda hine underfengon to hlaforde, Peohtas and
Bryttas, Scottas and Angle, swa swa se ælmihtiga God hi
90 geanlæhte to ðam for Oswoldes geearnungum þe hine æfre
wurðode. He fulworhte on Eferwic þæt ænlice mynster

79 *sandum*] U; *sande* A, -*e* on erasure of two letters by rev. 84
næfre added above *brosnunge* in U. *brosnunge*] AU, in A -*e* on erasure
by rev. *þes gebletsode swyðra*] *þeos gebletsode swyðre hand* A, -*eos* of
þeos on erasure, -*e* of *swyðre* on erasure, and *hand* inserted above
the line, all by rev.; *þys gebletsoda hand* U. 86 *swiðre*] AU, in A -*e* on
erasure by rev. (?). *gesundful*] A; *gesund* U. 87 *gerymed*] A; *getry-
med* U.

---

79 *sandum*: for the use of the plural see BT and Sup. s.v. *sand* f. II.
80 *het toceorfan*: the indef. object ('someone', 'men') of *hatan* in the
sense 'command' is not expressed, so that the dependent inf. appears
to be passive, 'he commanded the dish to be cut in pieces, and to be
given etc'; cp also l. 134 below, II 103, 178, 194, and *Primer* § 95.
83 *cwæðende*: for *cweðende*, see Intro. p. 7.
84 *þes . . . swyðra*: it seems reasonably certain that this was the
original reading of A (cp textual notes); for *swiðra*, 'right hand', see
BT and Sup. s.v. *swiþ* II 2 and cp LS X 31 and v.l.
84 *gebletsode*: nom.sg.m.def. (wk.), see Intro. p. 10.
85 f *his swiðre hand*: Bede here and at ll. 135 ff below speaks of both
hands: the alteration may have been made to make the correspond-
ence between the prophecy and its fulfilment more exact (cp Plum-
mer II 141).
91 *He fulworhte . . .* 92 *hæfde*: from Bede HE ii 14 (p. 114), or
ii 20 (p. 125). A *mynster* (Lat. *monasterium*) was a church with a
sufficient endowment to support a number of clergy to maintain its

þe his mæg Eadwine ær begunnon hæfde; and he swanc
for heofonan rice mid singalum gebedum swiþor þonne
he hogode hu he geheolde on worulde þa hwilwendlican
geþincðu þe he hwonlice lufode. He wolde æfter uhtsange ₉₅
oftost hine gebiddan and on cyrcan standan on syndrigum
gebedum of sunnan upgange mid swyðlicre onbryrdnysse;
and swa hwær swa he wæs he wurðode æfre God, up awendum
handbredum wiþ heofon[a]s weard.

93 *singalum*] AU, in A *a* altered from another letter. 94 *geheolde*]
A; *heolde* U. 99 *þæs* inserted after *wiþ* in A by rev.; om. U. *heof-
onas*] *heofones* AU, in A second *e* on erasure by rev.

---

services, whether or not the clergy lived under monastic rule. Ælfric
occasionally uses the terms *munuclif* (e.g. III 372) and *preostlif*
(LS XXXI 846; cp III 22, 24n) to refer to these two kinds of *mynster*.
Either kind of *mynster* might be, but of course neither was neces-
sarily, a cathedral.

92 *begunnon:* p.pt., see Intro. p. 11.

92 *he swanc . . . 99 weard:* Bede HE iii 12 (p. 151).

95 *He wolde . . . 97 onbryrdnysse:* Bede has *a tempore matutinae
laudis saepius ad diem usque in orationibus persteterit,* which probably
means that he stood praying from first light, when Lauds began,
until sunrise; less probably, from sunrise, when Lauds ended, until
full light of day. Ælfric's phrase *of sunnan upgange* can only mean
'from sunrise'; the phrase *æfter uhtsange* is ambiguous: *uhtsang*
usually means Nocturns (the night office, sung at about 2 a.m. in
summer, followed almost immediately by Lauds, and at about 3 a.m.
in winter, followed, before Lauds, by an interval devoted to reading);
but it may also mean Lauds (see PMLA x (1895) 145), and must do
so here, if, as seems likely, *æfter uhtsange* is synonymous with *of
sunnan upgange;* (cp also the version of this passage and the one
quoted below in the OE Bede (ed. Schipper 245/1287 ff, and 443/
2533 f)). Bede uses almost the same expression of St Audrey at HE
iv 17: *semper . . . ex tempore matutinae synaxeos, usque ad ortum diei,
in ecclesia precibus intenta persteterit,* which may have suggested
to Ælfric the addition of *on cyrcan* in the present passage.

98 f *up awendum handbredum:* dat. absolute, on which see QW
§§ 111, 152, etc; further examples occur at II 32, III 85.

99 *heofonas:* in all probability this was the original reading of A
(cp textual notes); see BT s.v. *wiþ* IX (1b) and cp CH II 182/16 and
LS III 451.

00 On þam ylcan timan com eac sum bisceop fram Rome-
byrig, Birinus gehaten, to Westsexena kyninge, Cynegyls
gehaten, se wæs ðagit hæðen, and eall Westsexena land.
Birinus witodlice gewende fram Rome be ðæs papan ræde
þe ða on Rome wæs, and behet þæt he wolde Godes willan
05 gefremman and bodian þam hæþenum þæs Hælendes naman
and þone soðan geleafan on fyrlenum landum. Þa becom he
to Westseaxan þe wæs ðagyt hæþen, and gebigde þone
cynincg Kynegyls to Gode, and ealle his leode to geleafan
mid him. Hit gelamp þa swa þæt se geleaffulla Oswold,
10 Norðhymbra cyning, wæs cumen to Cynegylse and hine to
fulluhte nam, fægen his gecyrrednysse. Þa geafon þa cynegas,
Cynegyls and Oswold, þam halgan Birine, him to bisceop-

---

102 *hæðen*] AU, in A preceded by erasure of one letter. 103 *rome*]
A; *rome byrig* U. *Honorivs* in margin of U. 108 *and cwichel* in margin
of U, marked for insertion after *kynegils*. 109 *swa*] A; om. U.

---

100 *on þam ylcan . . . 119 gyt:* from Bede HE iii 7 (first part only;
the remainder of this chapter, and the whole of the next, which is
also omitted by Ælfric, are not concerned with St Oswald). Bede
gives no dates. The Chronicle (all MSS) records Birinus' mission under
634; the baptism of Cynegyls under 635; of his son Cwichelm, who
apparently reigned jointly with him (see Plummer II 98), under 636
(it is uncertain where the writer of the marginal note in U obtained his
information); and of Cuðred, Cwichelm's son, under 639; 'but', says
Plummer, 'considering how [the chronicler] has blundered over other
dates it is not possible to feel much confidence here' (ii 20 f). Accord-
ing to the Chronicle (all MSS) Cynegyls began to reign in 611, and
reigned for 31 years; but his death is placed under 641 (BCEF)
or 643 (A).

101, 102 *Westsexena:* on the LWS 'smoothing' see Campbell § 312.

103 *ðæs papan:* Honorius I (625–38): his name is given by Bede
and in Chron. E s.a. 634; which, if either, is the source of the
information in the marginal note in U is not clear.

107 *Westseaxan:* historically dat.pl., see Intro. p. 10; but the sg.vb.
in the rel. clause following, suggests that it may no longer have been
felt to be a pl., i.e. had become a purely territorial designation; cp
Myrcan l. 147 below, and Sweet's *Reader* (1946) XV 107n.

110 f *hine to fulluhte nam:* i.e. was his sponsor, godfather.

111 *cynegas:* on the loss of *n*, which occurs occasionally in plural
forms in A (beside normal *cyningas, -a, -um*), see Campbell § 474(5).

stole, þa burh Dorcanceaster; and he þærbinnan wunode, Godes lof arærende, and gerihtlæcende þæt folc mid lare to geleafan, to langum fyrste, oð þæt he gesælig siþode to 115 Criste; and his lic wearþ bebyrged on ðære ylcan byrig, oð þæt Hædde bisceop eft his ban ferode to Wintanceastre and mid wurðmynte gelogode binnan Ealdan Mynstre, þær man hine wurðað gyt.

Hwæt þa Oswold cyning his cynedom geheold hlisful- 120 lice for worulde and mid micclum geleafan and on eallum dædum his Drihten arwurðode, oð þæt he ofslagen wearð for his folces ware on þam nigoðan geare þe he rices geweold, þa þa he sylf wæs on yld[e] eahta and þrittig geare. Hit gewearð swa be þam þæt him wann on Penda, Myrcena 125

123 geweold] AU, in A ge inserted by original scribe. 124 wæs on ylde] A, -e by rev. (on erasure?); on ylde wæs U. geare] A, altered to geara by rev.; geara U.

---

113 Dorcanceaster: Dorchester-on-Thames, near Oxford; the West Saxon see was later transferred to Winchester: the circumstances are related in the latter part of Bede's chapter.

115 oð þæt . . . 116 Criste: Birinus' death is variously placed between 648 and 650 (see Plummer II 143).

117 Hædde: bishop of Winchester from 676 to 705 (Chron. (all MSS) 703). The translation of Birinus' remains was clearly due to the removal of the West Saxon see to Winchester.

118 Ealdan Mynstre: the cathedral church of St Peter and St Paul, founded by Cenwalh, son and successor of Cynegyls; so called to distinguish it from the New Minster, on which see III 95n. See also III 116–17n.

118 þær . . . 119 gyt: Ælfric's addition.

120 Hwæt þa . . . 130 Cristenan: from Bede HE iii 9.

122 oð þæt . . . 123 geweold: the nine years of Oswald's reign were reckoned from the death of Edwin, since it was generally agreed, according to Bede, ut nomen et memoria apostatarum de catalogo regum Christianorum prorsus aboleri deberet, neque aliquis regno eorum annus adnotari (HE iii 9, p. 145; cp iii 1, p. 128, and above l. 52 note). The day of Oswald's death was August 5, the day for which Ælfric's homily was written (but only U has the correct rubric: Nonas A[u]gusti. passio (Natale A, and, according to Wanley, V) Sancti oswaldi Regis et martiris; cp also III 3 f note).

124 geare: gen.pl., see Intro. p. 10, and cp textual notes.

125, 127 Penda: king of Mercia 632–54 (see Stenton 81 ff); on his attitude to Christianity ibid. 120, and on his career generally ibid. 38 f.

cyning, þe æt his mæges slege ær, Eadwines cyninges,
Cedwallan fylste; and se Penda ne cuðe þe Criste nan þincg,
and eall Myrcena folc wæs ungefullod þagit. Hi comon þa to
gefeohte to Maserfelda begen and fengon togædere oð þæt
130 þær feollon þa Cristenan and þa hæðenan genealæhton to
þam halgan Oswolde. þa geseah he genealecan his lifes
geendunge and gebæd for his folc þe þær feallende sweolt
and betæhte heora sawla, and hine sylfne, Gode, and þus
clypode on his fylle, 'God gemiltsa urum sawlum!' þa het
135 se hæþena cynincg his heafod of aslean, and his swiðran
earm, and settan hi to myrcelse. þa æfter Oswoldes slege
feng Oswig his broðor to Norðhymbra rice, and rad mid
werode to þær his broðor heafod stod on stacan gefæstnod,
and genam þæt heafod and his swiðran hand, and mid
140 arwurðnysse ferode to Lindisfarnea cyrcan. þa wearð
gefylled, swa we her foresædon, þæt his swiðre hand wunað
hal mid þam flæsce butan ælcere brosnunge swa se bisceop
gecwæð. Se earm wearþ geled arwurðlice on scrine of seolfre

127 *cedwallan*] A, altered to *ceadwallan* by rev.; *Cedwealla* U. 128
ungefullod] A; *unfullod* U. 135 *aslean*] AU, in A *n* altered from *h*;
slean V. 136 *hi*] AV; *him* U. *þa*] AU; *þa* V. 138 *stod on stacan*] AU;
on stacan [*stod*] V. 143 *gecwæð*] AUV, in A *ge* inserted by original
scribe. *geled*] A, second *e* altered from *æ*; *geledd* U.

129 *Maserfelda:* now Oswestry (Shropshire), < *Oswoldes treo*, cp
the Welsh name of the place, Croes Oswallt; for the OE name see
Holthausen, *Ae. etym. Wörterbuch*, 428.

130 *and þa hæðenan* . . . 140 *cyrcan:* from Bede HE iii 12.

131 *genealecan:* for *-læcan*, see Intro. p. 7.

132 *sweolt:* 3 sg.pret.ind. from *sweltan:* invariably thus in A, but
the regular form is *swealt*.

135 f *his swiðran earm*, 139 *his swiðran hand*, etc; see above
l. 85 f note.

137 *Oswig:* Oswi (or Osweo), king of Bernicia only from 641 to 654,
and of all Northumbria from 654 to 670.

140 *Lindisfarnea:* of (i.e. on) the island of Lindisfarne, now Holy
Island, off the coast of Northumberland. It was given by Oswald to
Aidan as his see (HE iii 3), and it continued an episcopal see (with
one short interruption, from 664 to 667), until the viking invasion of
Northumbria in 875 (see Plummer ii 89 f). For the form of the second
element of the name see Campbell § 238(2) and fn. 2.

140 *þa wearð* . . . 146 *wæs:* from Bede HE iii 6.

asmiþod on Sancte Petres mynstre binnan Bebbanbyrig þe
þære sæ strande and lið þær swa andsund swa he of aslagen 145
wæs.

His broþor dohtor eft siððan on Myrcan wearð cwen and
geaxode his ban and gebrohte hi to Lindesige to Bardanige
mynstre, þe heo micclum lufode; ac þa mynstermenn noldon
for menniscum gedwylde þone sanct underfon, ac man sloh 150
an geteld ofer þa halgan ban binnan þære licreste. Hwæt þa

---

144 *mynstre*] AV; *cyrcan* U. *bebbanbyrig*] AUV, in A *e* altered
from *æ*. 145 *aslagen*] AV; *slagen* U. 148 *bardanige*] AV, in A *d* on
erasure (by rev.?); *beardanige* U. 151 *licreste*] AUV, in A first *e*
altered from *æ*.

---

144 *Sancte: sanct* (m.) is usually declined according to the general
m.decl., but beside the normal gen. *sanctes* (II 196, etc), a gen. *sancte*,
as here, also occurs. It represents a direct OE development of the
Lat. gen.sg.m. *sancti*, and Ælfric appears to use it only as here
without the def.art. before a proper name (so also II 2; III 117); see
Sweet's *Reader* (1946) XV 144n, and cp II 216–17n below.

144 *Bebbanbyrig*: now Bamburgh, on the coast of Northumberland,
not far south of Holy Island. It was the chief stronghold of the early
Bernician kingdom.

147 *His broþor dohtor . . .* 165 *wæron gedrehte*: from Bede HE iii 11
(first half: the second part, relating the cure of a demoniac, is
omitted).

147 *His broþor dohtor . . . cwen*: Osthryth, daughter of Oswald's
brother Oswi (see above l. 137n) and wife of Æthelræd, king of
Mercia 675–704. *Myrcan*: historically dat.pl., see Intro. p. 10, and
above l. 107n.

148 *geaxode his ban*: probably Oswald's body had been buried on
the battlefield. The translation to Bardney must have taken place
some time between 675 (the date of Æthelræd's accession) and 697
(the date of Osthryth's death).

148 *Lindesige*: the ancient kingdom of Lindsey, corresponding
roughly to the division of the modern county of Lincoln, called the
Parts of Lindsey; on its history in the seventh century, see Plummer
II 155.

148 *Bardanige*: Bardney, Lincolnshire; see Intro. p. 4, fn. 1.

150 *for menniscum gedwylde*: *quia etsi sanctum eum nouerant, tamen
quia de alia prouincia ortus fuerat, et super eos regnum acceperat,
ueteranis eum odiis etiam mortuum insequebantur* (Bede HE iii 11; cp
Plummer's note II 155).

God geswutelode þæt he halig sanct wæs, swa þæt heofon[lic]
leoht ofer þæt geteld astreht stod up to heofonum, swilce
healic sunnbeam, ofer ealle ða niht; and þa leoda beheoldon
55 geond ealle þa scire swiðe wundrigende. þa wurdon þa
mynstermen micclum afyrhte and bædon þæs on mergen
þæt hi moston þone sanct mid arwurðnysse underfon, þone
þe hi ær forsocon. þa ðwoh man þa halgan ban and bær
into þære cyrcan arwurðlice on scrine and gelogodon hi upp;
60 and þær wurdon gehælede þurh his halgan geearnunge fela
mettrume menn fram mislicum coþum. þæt wæter þe man
þa ban mid aþwoh binnan þære cyrcan wearð agoten swa on
anre hyrnan; and seo eorðe siþþan þe þæt wæter underfeng,
wearð manegum to bote. Mid þam duste wurdon afligde
65 deofla fram mannum þa þe on wodnysse ær wæron gedrehte.

Eac swilce þær he feol on þam gefeohte ofslagen, men
namon þa eorðan to adligum mannum and dydon on wæter

152 *heofonlic*] U; *heofon* AV, in A altered to *heofonlic* by rev. 153
geteld] AUV, in A erasure (of two letters ?) before *t. astreht*] AUV,
in A *e* altered from *æ*. 159 *gelogodon*] AV; *gelogode* U. 165 *wodnysse*]
AU, in A *d* on erasure (by rev.?); *wohnysse* V.

152 *heofonlic leoht:* I have adopted the reading of U, with which
the emendation of the reviser of A coincides (cp textual notes and
Introduction p. 4). The omission of *-lic* may have been induced by
the initial *l-* of the following word. It should be noticed, however,
that the only occurrence in prose of a compound *heofonleoht* recorded
in BT (apart from the present passage), is from the OE Bede, where
it translates *lux caelestis* in the rubric to the chapter from which the
present passage is taken; it is otherwise only recorded from *Andreas*
974. There is however no indication elsewhere in the homily that
Ælfric was influenced by the OE version of Bede's HE, although he
certainly knew of it (see Intro. p. 18, fn. 3).

159 *gelogodon:* on the pl.vb. see QW § 126, and cp II 174, III 222;
the apparently sg. form in U—which would be more strictly gram-
matical—may be due to weakening of the unstressed syllable (cp
Intro. p. 6, fn. 4).

160 *geearnunge:* acc.pl., see Intro. p. 10.

165 *deofla:* neut.pl., see Intro. p. 10.

165 *wodnysse:* cp textual notes and Intro. p. 4, fn. 1; Bede has *ipsa
terra . . . ad abigendos ex obsessis corporibus daemones gratiae salutaris
haberet effectum.*

166 *Eac . . . 182 dyde:* from Bede HE iii 9.

wanhalum to þicgenne and hi wurdon gehælede þurh þone
halgan wer. Sum wegfarende man ferde wið þone feld; þa
wearð his hors gesicclod and sona þær feol, wealwigende 170
geond ða eorðan wodum gelicost; mid þam þe hit swa
wealweode geond þone widgillan feld, þa becom hit embe
lang þær se cynincg Oswold on þam gefeohte feoll, swa swa
we ær foresædan; and hit sona aras swa hit hrepode þa
stowe, hal eallum limum, and se hlaford þæs fægnode. Se 175
ridda þa ferde forð on his weg þider he gemynt hæfde; þa
wæs þær an mæden licgende on paralisyn lange gebrocod.
He began þa to reccenne hu him on rade getimode, and mann
ferode þæt mæden to þære foresædan stowe. Heo wearð þa
on slæpe and sona eft awoc, [an]sund eallum limum fram 180
þam egeslican broce: band þa hire heafod and bliðe ham
ferde, gangænde on fotum swa heo gefyrn ær ne dyde.

Eft siððan ferde eac sum ærendfæst ridda be ðære ylcan
stowe and geband on anum claþe of þam halgan duste þære
deorwurðan stowe and lædde forð mid him þær he fundode 185

169 *wegfarende*] A; *-ferende* UV. 170 *gesicclod*] A, second *c* altered
from another letter; *gesiclod* U; (*ge*)*sicelod* V. 172 *ferde* added in
margin of A after *feld* by rev.; UV om. *þa*] AV; *þa* U. 174 *ær*]
AV; *her* U. 176 *þa* (first)] AUV, in A inserted by original scribe.
þider] AV; *þyder ðe* U. 178 *reccenne*] AUV, in A *ge* prefixed by rev.
180 *ansund*] AU, in A *an* on erasure by rev.; *andsund* V. 183 *eac*]
AU; om. V.

169 *wegfarende :* see Intro. p. 4, fn. 3.
172 *wealweode :* for *wealwode* (as in UV); the form in A is perhaps
due to contamination with *eode*, pret. of *gan*.
174 *ær :* cp l. 141 above, and Assmann VI 138, which suggest that
U may have the better reading here; but *ær*, although with *foresecgan*
it seems redundant, is supported by Assmann IX 24. Cp also LS XXV
513 and v.l. *foresædan :* pret.pl., see Intro p. 10.
176 *þider :* the rel. 'whither' is either *þider* or *þider þe* in OE (cp
textual notes): it is not possible to decide which reading represents
the original here.
179 *heo :* masc. and fem. pronouns are sometimes used with refer-
ence to neuter nouns denoting human beings (cp QW § 124).
181 *band . . . heafod :* Bede has *crines conposuit, caput linteo
cooperuit.*
182 *gangænde :* for *-ende*, see Intro. p. 7, fn. 3.
183 *Eft . . . 196 gehwilcum :* from Bede HE iii 10.

39

to; þa gemette he gebeoras bliðe æt þam huse: he aheng þa
þæt dust on ænne heahne post and sæt mid þam gebeorum
blissigende samod. Man worhte þa micel fyr tomiddes ðam
gebeorum and þa spearcan wundon wið þæs rofes swyðe, oð
190 þæt þæt hus færlice eall on fyre wearð, and þa gebeoras
flugon afyrhte aweg. þæt hus wearþ ða forburnon buton
þam anum poste þe þæt halige dust on ahangen wæs: se post
ana ætstod ansund mid þam duste and hi swyðe wundroden
þæs halgan weres geearnunga þæt þæt fyr ne mihte þa
195 moldan forbærnan; and manega menn siððan gesohton þone
stede, heora hæle feccende, and heora freonda gehwilcum.

þa asprang his hlisa geond [þæt] land wide, and eac swilce
to Irlande, and eac suþ to Franclande, swa swa sum mæsse-
preost be anum men sæde. Se preost cwæð þæt an wer wære
200 on Irlande gelæred, se [ne] gymde his lare and he lithwon

190 *þæt þæt*] AV; *þæt* U. 192 *se*] AU; *Se* V. 193 *ana ætstod*] AV;
ætstod ana U. *wundroden*] AU, in A altered to *wundrodon* by rev.;
wundrodon V. 197 *þæt*] U; *þa* A. 199 *men*] AU, in A inserted by
original scribe. *cwæð*] A; *sæde* U. 200 *se . . . lare*] A, *ne* inserted
by rev.; U om. entire clause.

189 *wið þæs rofes:* Bede adds that it was of wattles, thatched with
straw; *rofes* for *hrofes*, see Intro. p. 9.

191 *forburnon:* p.pt., see Intro. p. 11.

193 *ana:* following a noun or pronoun (either immediately, as here,
or after an interval, as at III 183, 286), the adj. *an* means 'alone'.
Ælfric uses the form *ana* (occasionally *ane*, as at II 64), originally
the nom.sg.m.wk., as nom.sg. of all genders and as nom.pl.; the other
cases are strong (e.g. II 85, III 304). See also III 237n.

193 *wundroden:* pret.pl., see Intro. p. 10, and cp textual notes.

197 *þa asprang . . . 220 wundra:* from Bede HE iii 13.

197 *þæt land:* Bede has *Brittaniae fines . . . uniuersos*.

200 *se ne gymde his lare:* I have adopted the reviser's reading,
which gives a meaning closer to Bede's. At this point Bede has
*scolasticus quidam de genere Scottorum, doctus quidem uir studio
litterarum, sed erga curam perpetuae suae saluationis nihil omnino
studii et industriae gerens;* but Ælfric has combined with this a sub-
sequent passage in which the scholar says of himself, *tempore non
pauco inter studia diuinae lectionis, uitiorum potius inplicamentis,
quam diuinis solebam seruire mandatis.* It is possible, however, that
the original reading of A is the correct one, and means 'who gave (all)
his attention to, was engrossed in, his studies'.

hogode embe his sawle þearfa oððe his scyppendes beboda,
ac adreah his lif on dyslicum weorcum, oð ðæt he wearð
geuntrumod and to ende gebroht. þa clypode he þone
preost þe hit cydde eft þus, and cwæð him to sona mid
sarlicre stemne, 'Nu ic sceall geendian earmlicum deaþe and 205
to helle faran for fracodum dædum, [n]u wolde ic gebetan
gif ic abidan moste, and to Gode gecyrran and to godum
þeawum, and min lif awendan eall to Godes willan; and ic
wat þæt ic ne eom wyrðe þæs fyrstes, buton sum halga me
þingie to þam hælende Criste. Nu is us gesæd þæt sum halig 210
cyning is on eowrum earde Oswold gehaten: nu gif þu ænig
þincg hæfst of þæs halgan reliquium, syle me, ic þe bidde.'
Ða sæde se preost him, 'Ic hæbbe of þam stocce þe his
heafod on stod and gif þu gelyfan wylt, þu wurþ[e]st hal
sona.' Hwæt þa se mæssepreost þæs mannes ofhreow and 215
scof on halig wæter of þam halgan treowe: sealde þam
adligan of to supenne, and he sona gewyrpte and syððan
leofode lange on worulde and gewende to Gode mid eallra
heortan and mid halgum weorcum and swa hwider swa he
com, he cydde þas wundra. For þy ne sceall nan mann 220
awægan þæt he sylfwylles behæt þam ælmihtigan Gode

201 *þearfa*] A, altered to *þearfe* by rev.; *þearfe* U. 202 *adreah*] AU,
first *a* inserted by original scribe in both. 203 *he*] AU, in A inserted
by original scribe. 206 *nu*] U; *Nu* A. 210 *þingie*] A; *geðingige* U.
214 *wurþest*] A, *e* on erasure by rev.; *wyrst* U. 218 *eallra*] A, altered
to *eallre* by rev.; *ealre* U.

201 *þearfa*: acc.sg., see Intro. p. 10, and cp textual notes. *beboda*:
neut.pl., see Intro. p. 10.
205 *Nu* . . . 206 *nu*: correlative conj. and adv. (cp textual notes).
214 *wurþest*: 2 sg.pres.ind.: the regular form is *wyrst*, as in U;
the corrected form in A is clearly an analogical formation based on
the inf.stem, but if the original scribe wrote *wurþast*, the form may
be due to confusion with *wurðian*, cons.(wk.) vb. (2).
215 *ofhreow*: this appears to be Ælfric's usual form of the 3 sg.
pret.ind. of *ofhreowan*; see BT and Sup. s.v. and cp SB § 126 Anm.2.
218 *eallra*: dat.sg.f., see Intro. p. 10, and cp textual notes.
220 *wundra*: acc.pl., see Intro. p. 10: the nom. and acc.pl. of this
word, which occurs frequently, invariably takes this form.
220 *For þy* . . . 223 *þæt*: Ælfric's addition.

þonne he adlig bið, þe læs þe he sylf losige gif he alihð Gode
þæt.

Nu cwæð se halga Beda, þe ðas boc gedihte, þæt hit nan
225 wundor nys þæt se halga cynincg untrumnysse g[e]hæle nu he
on heofonum [leo]fað, for ðan þe he wolde gehelpan, þa þa he
her on life wæs, þearfum and wannhalum and him bigwiste
syllan. Nu hæfð he þone wurðmynt on þære ecan worulde
mid þam ælmihtigan Gode for his godnysse. Eft se halga
230 Cuðberht, þa þa he git cnapa wæs, geseah hu Godes ænglas
feredon Aidanes sawle, þæs halgan bisceopes, bliðe to heo-
fonum to þam ecan wuldre þe he on worulde geearnode.

Þæs halgan Oswoldes ban wurdon eft gebroht æfter
manegum gearum to Myrcena lande into Gleawceastre, and
235 God þær geswutelode oft fela wundra þurh þone halgan wer.
Sy þæs wuldor þam Ælmihtigan a to worulde. Amen.

225 *gehæle*] AU, in A first *e* by rev. on erasure. 226 *leofað*] AU, in A
leo on erasure by rev. 230 *godes*] A; om. U. 234 *manegum*] AU, in A
a altered (from *æ*?). 235 *fela*] AU, in A altered to *feala* by rev. 236
ælmihtigan] A, after which rev. has inserted *gode*. *ðe on ecnysse
rixað*; *ælmihtigan gode* U. *to worulde*] A; *to worolde world* U.

224 *þæt hit . . . 229 godnysse*: from Bede HE iii 9 (p. 145), and 12
(p. 151).

226 *leofað*: the original scribe probably wrote *lyfað*, although in the
2, 3, sg.pres.ind. of this vb., back mutation is usual in other homilies
in A.

229 *Eft . . . 232 geearnode*: Cuthbert, the celebrated Northumbrian
saint, died in 687. The story of Aidan's vision is told by Bede in his
Life of St Cuthbert c. 4 (ed. Bertram Colgrave, *Two Lives of Saint
Cuthbert* (Cambridge, 1940) 164 ff), in the anonymous life Bk. I
c. V (*ib*. 68 ff), and by Ælfric CH II 136.

230 *ænglas*: for *englas*, see Intro. p. 7.

231 *Aidanes . . . bisceopes*: see III 82n.

233 *þæs halgan . . . 235 wer*: Ælfric's addition. Oswald's remains
were translated to Gloucester by Æthelræd, aldorman of Mercia, and
his wife Æthelflæd, into the new monastery which they had founded
there in his honour: the translation is recorded in the Chron. s.a.
909C, 906D. At Bardney, in territory settled by the Danes in 877, the
relics were in the hands of men who were still heathen.

II

ST EDMUND, KING AND MARTYR

Sum swyðe gelæred munuc com suþan ofer sæ fram
Sancte Benedictes stowe on Æþelredes cynincges dæge to
Dunstane ærcebisceope þrim gearum ær [þam þe] he
forðferde, and se munuc hatte Abbo; þa wurdon hi æt
spræce oþ þæt Dunstan rehte be Sancte Eadmunde, swa swa   5
Eadmundes swurdbora hit rehte Æþelstane cynincge, þa þa
Dunstan iung man wæs and se swurdbora wæs forealdod
man. þa gesette se munuc ealle þa gereccednysse on anre bec
and eft, ða þa seo boc com to us binnan feawum gearum, þa
awende we hit on Englisc, swa swa hit heræfter stent. Se 10
munuc þa, Abbo, binnan twam gearum gewende ham to his
mynstre and wearð sona to abbode geset on þam ylcan
mynstre.

Eadmund se eadiga, Eastengla cynincg, wæs snotor and

1–13 *Sum . . . mynstre*] ABO; om. U. 2 *cynincges dæge*] AO;
dagum kynges B. 3 *þam þe*] B; om. A; O illegible, but there is suffi-
cient room. 4 *se*] AO; *sum* B. 4 f *æt spræce*] A; *on spece* B. 8 *þa*] A;
þas B. 11 *his*] A; om. B. 12 *sona*] AO; *þa* B.

1 *Sum . . . 13 mynstre:* see Intro. pp. 18 f.

2 *Sancte Benedictes stowe:* the monastery of Fleury, near Orléans
(now called St-Benoît-sur-Loire). The remains of St Benedict had
been removed there from their burial place at Monte Cassino c. 673
(see Dom Justin McCann, *Saint Benedict* (1939) chap. XIV). On the
form *sancte* see I 144n.

3 *ær þam þe: ær* alone is used as a conj. in OE, but not normally in
LS.

4 *þa wurdon . . . 8 bec:* from Abbo's Dedicatory Epistle.

10 *hit:* neut. pronouns are occasionally used with reference to
masc. and fem. nouns denoting inanimate objects (cp *Primer* § 84).

14 *Eadmund . . . 24 geleafan:* the description of King Edmund's
character is drawn from Abbo III and IV. Abbo's general historical
introduction (I and II), and the account in III of Edmund's ancestry
and the circumstances of his election to the kingdom, are omitted.
Abbo gives no dates; later writers place Edmund's accession in 855,
in his fourteenth year. Nothing certain is known of the condition of
East Anglia at this time (cp Plummer ii 61 f).

15 wurðful and wurðode symble mid æþelum þeawum þone
ælmihtigan God. He wæs eadmod and geþungen and swa
anræde þurhwunode þæt he nolde abugan to bysmorfullum
leahtrum, ne on naþre healfe he ne ahylde his þeawas, ac
wæs symble gemyndig þære soþan lare, 'þu eart to heafod-
20 men geset? ne ahefe þu ðe, ac beo betwux mannum swa swa
an man of him'. He wæs cystig wædlum and wydewum swa
swa fæder and mid welwillendnysse gewissode his folc symle
to rihtwisnysse and þam reþum styrde and gesæliglice
leofode on soþan geleafan.

25   Hit gelamp ða æt nextan þæt þa Deniscan leode ferdon
mid sciphere hergiende and sleande wide geond land swa

16 *He*] AOU; *he* B. 18 *naþre*] AOU; *nane* B. *ahylde*] AU; *ahydde*
B. 19 *lare*] AU; *lufe* B. *þu*] AU; *gyf þu* B. 21 *He*] AOU; *he* B. 24
on soþan geleafan] AU; om. B, and (probably) O. 25 *Hit*] AU; *hit* B.

18 *ne . . . þeawas:* Abbo (IV) has, *nec declinabat ad dexteram,
extollendo se de meritis, nec ad sinistram, succumbendo vitiis humanæ
fragilitatis.*

19 *þu eart . . . 21 of him:* Ecclesiasticus 32¹ (as quoted by Abbo),
*Principem te constituerunt? noli extolli, sed esto in illis quasi unus ex
illis.*

24 *soþan:* dat.sg.m. indefinite (strong), see Intro. p. 10.

25 *Hit gelamp . . . 33 rowende,* 35 *se foresæda . . . 38 cristenan:*
Abbo V, omitting ll. 1–27 (more than half), which describe the savage
character of the Northern peoples.

26 *sciphere:* the great viking army, which was to spend fourteen
years ravaging this country, and which eventually occupied large
areas of northern and eastern England; it arrived here in the autumn
of 865 (Chron., s.a. 866, see A. H. Smith, *The Parker Chronicle* (1939)
note ad.loc.). Ælfric (l. 29 below) follows Abbo in placing the first
landing in Northumbria; according to the Chron. it was in East
Anglia, whence the Norsemen moved to Northumbria in the autumn
of 866; they returned to East Anglia in 869. There are further dis-
crepancies with the account of the events of 869 in the Chron. (which
is here only very little later than the events it records). The most im-
portant is that the Chron. states (s.a. 870) that Edmund fought
against the invaders (cp ll. 88 ff below). It also says that the vikings
had come overland through Mercia (cp l. 33 below), and had taken
winter quarters at Thetford (while Abbo suggests (VI 18 ff) that they
remained close to their ships). It may be that there is some confusion
in Abbo's account between the first and second viking invasions of
East Anglia.

44

swa heora gewuna is. On þam flotan wæron þa fyrmestan
heafodmen Hinguar and Hubba, geanlæhte þurh deofol,
and hi on Norðhymbra lande gelendon mid æscum and
aweston þæt land and þa leoda ofslogon. Þa gewende ₃₀

27 *fyrmestan*] AU; *fyrstan* B.

28 *Hinguar:* ON *Ívarr*; in English records the name occurs in
various forms: *Ingwær, Inwær, Iwer, Igwar*, etc; the form used by
Abbo is *Inguar*; in the MSS of Ælfric's homily the spelling varies
between *Hinguar* and *Hingwar*. The Alfredian Chron. does not state
who the leaders of the Great Army were, but the way in which
Inwær is mentioned s.a. 878, clearly indicates that he was a well-
known figure in it. The chronicler Æthelweard, writing more than a
hundred years later, at about the same time as Abbo, recording the
arrival of the army, calls it *classes tyranni Igwares*. According to
Æthelweard he died in the same year as Edmund. He is probably to
be identified with the viking whom the Irish annalists call *Imhar*,
whose activities they record from 852 till his death, which they place
in 873, when they call him 'King of all the Norsemen of all Ireland
and Britain'. Later he is stated to be a son of the celebrated viking
Ragnar Lothbrok: at the beginning of the twelfth century, for
example, the Icelandic historian Ari Thorgilsson dates the settle-
ment of Iceland at the time of the death of St Edmund—*i þann
tíð . . . er Ívarr Ragnars sonr loðbrókar lét drepa Eadmund hinn helga
Engla konung.* The earliest mention of the relationship is made by
Adam of Bremen (*c.* 1075). Later Norse sources call him *Ívarr
beinlausi*, 'the Boneless'. For a survey of the evidence relating to
Ragnar and his sons, see A. Mawer, 'Ragnar Lothbrok and his Sons',
Saga-Book of the Viking Club vi (1908–9) 68–89, and A. H. Smith,
'The Sons of Ragnar Lothbrok', *ibid.* xi (1928–36) 173–91; and cp
Grant Loomis, 'Saint Edmund and the Lodbrok Legend', HSN xv
(1933) 1–23.

28 *Hubba:* ON *Ubbi.* Abbo's is the earliest mention of him. The
mid-eleventh century *Historia de Sancto Cuthberto* names as the
leaders of the Great Army, *Ubba dux Fresonum et Healfdena rex
Denorum* (ed. T. Arnold, R.S. 75 (1882–5) i 204, cp 202). At a later
date he too is enrolled among the numerous sons of Ragnar: the first
allusion to the relationship is in the *Annals of St Neots* (*c.* 1125),
where we are told that the raven-banner of the vikings, captured in
878, was woven by *tres sorores Hynguari et Hubbae, filiae videlicet
Lodebrochi* (ed. W. H. Stevenson (1904) 138). Cp references cited in
the preceding note.

29 *æscum:* in this sense 'the OE word is an anglicizing of ON *askr*'
(E. V. Gordon, *The Battle of Maldon* (1949) l. 69n.).

Hinguar east mid his scipum and Hubba belaf on Norðhym-
bra lande, gewunnenum sige mid wælhreownysse. Hinguar
þa becom to Eastenglum rowende, on þam geare þe Ælfred
æðelincg an and twentig geare wæs, se þe Westsexena
35 cynincg siþþan wearð mære; and se foresæda Hinguar
færlice swa swa wulf on lande bestalcode and þa leode
[of]sloh, wæras and wif and þa unwittigan cild, and to
bysmore tucode þa bilewitan cristenan.

He sende ða sona syððan to þam cyninge beotlic ærende

31 *scipum*] ABU, in A *s* altered from *c* by original scribe. 33 *þa
becom*] AOU; *bicom þa* B. 36 *on lande*] A; *to lande* BOU. 37 *ofsloh*] U;
sloh AB, in A preceded by erasure of *of*. 39 *sona syððan*] A; *syððan
sona* BU.

32 *gewunnenum sige:* see I 98 f note.

33 *on þam geare . . .* 35 *mære:* not in Abbo, who gives no indica-
tion of the year. Ælfric's authority for the statement is not known
(cp Asser, s.a. 870 (ed. W. H. Stevenson (1904) 26), Simeon of Dur-
ham, *Historia Regum*, s.a. 870 (ed. T. Arnold, R.S. 75 (1882-5) ii 76);
nor is it clear what year he meant to indicate by it. The viking inva-
sion of E. Anglia and the death of Edmund are recorded in the Chron.
s.a. 870, i.e. they occurred between Sept. 869 and Sept. 870; since
Edmund's death occurred on Nov. 20, they must have occurred in
869 (cp A. H. Smith, *The Parker Chronicle*, 870n). According to the
regnal lists Alfred was turned 23 when he succeeded to the kingdom
(in April 871), which would put his birth between April 847 and
April 848. This, however, cannot be reconciled with the date given
by Asser, 849, even if Asser's year 849 started (as it may have done)
in the September of (what we should call) 848. If Ælfric is referring
to the actual date of the viking invasion, his evidence (for what it
may be worth) would support the year 848 as the year of King
Alfred's birth; if, however (like most later chroniclers) he is referring
to the year 870, clearly it would support 849. See also Plummer ii
79; Stevenson, *op.cit.*, 152, 181.

34 *geare:* gen.pl., see Intro. p. 10.

36 *swa swa wulf:* Abbo VI ll. 20 ff.

36 *on lande bestalcode:* the verb does not occur elsewhere, so that it
is impossible to decide whether the prep. following it should be *on* or
to (cp textual notes); the derived noun *stalcung* occurs CH II 138/6.

37 *wæras:* for *weras*, see Intro. p. 7.

39 *He sende . . .* 48 *wiðstandan:* from Abbo VII (VI, in which
Hinguar inquires of the king's whereabouts, and which contains
further references to the character of the Danes, is omitted).

þæt he abugan sceolde to his manrædene gif he rohte his ⁴⁰
feores. Se ærendraca com þa to Eadmunde cynincge and
Hingwares ærende him ardlice abead: 'Hingwar ure cyning,
cene and sigefæst on sæ and on lande, hæfð fela leoda
gewyld and com nu mid fyrde færlice her to lande þæt he her
wintersetl mid his werode hæbbe. Nu het he þe dælan þine ⁴⁵
digelan goldhordas and þinre yldrena gestreon ardlice wið
hine, and þu beo his underkyning, gif ðu cucu beon wylt, for
ðan þe ðu næfst þa mihte þæt þu mage him wiðstandan.'
    Hwæt þa Eadmund [cyning] clypode ænne bisceop þe him
þa gehendost wæs, and wið hine smeade hu he þam reþan ⁵⁰
Hingware andwyrdan sceolde. Þa forhtode se bisceop for
þam færlican gelimpe and for þæs cynincges life, and cwæð
þæt him ræd þuhte þæt he to þam gebuge þe him bead
Hinguar. Þa suwode se cynincg and beseah to þære eorþan,
and cwæð þa æt nextan cynelice him to, 'Eala þu bisceop, ⁵⁵

---

40 f *rohte his feores*] A; *his feores rohte* BOU. 42 *ardlice*] AOU;
heardlice B. 43 *hæfð*] ABO; *he hæfð* U. *leoda*] AU; *þeodæ* B. 45
Nu] ABO; *nu* U. 46 *þinre*] A, altered to *þinra* by rev.; *þinra* OU;
þine B. *ardlice*] AOU; *hærlice* B. 47 *and*] AU; *þæt* B. 49 *eadmund*]
AB, in a second *d* inserted by original scribe; *eamund* U. *cyning*]
OBU; om. A. 51 *andwyrdan*] AU; *berstan* B. *Þa*] AU; *þa* B.
53 f *him bead hinguar*] AOU; *hinguar him bead* B.

---

45 *het*: for *hæt(t)*, 3 sg.pres.ind., see Intro. p. 7.

46 *þinre*: gen.pl., see Intro. p. 10, and cp textual notes.

47 *and þu beo*: sc. *þæt* before *þu*: *hatan* is followed by a dependent
inf. (e.g. III 284; cp I 8on), or a *þæt*-clause (with subj.) (e.g. III 31,
310 f): here the two constructions are mixed. It is possible, however,
that B has the correct reading. Abbo has, . . . *mandat ut cum eo
antiquos thesauros et paternas divitias sub eo regnaturus dividas.*

49 *Hwæt þa . . . 71 lybbe ic*: from Abbo VIII.

49 *ænne bisceop*: up to the time of the Danish invasion there were
two bishoprics in E. Anglia, one of Norfolk with a cathedral at
Elmham, the other of Suffolk, with a cathedral at Dunwich. The
bishop of Elmham at this time was Humberht, and the bishop of
Dunwich, Æthelwald. If Edmund was staying near Norwich (see
138 f note), it would seem most probable that the bishop summoned
by him was Humberht. According to Simeon of Durham, Humberht
was martyred with Edmund (ed. T. Arnold, R.S. 75 (1882-5) i 55, ii
107).

to bysmore synd getawode þas earman landleoda, and me
nu leofre wære þæt ic on [ge]feohte feolle, wið þam þe min
folc moste heora eardes brucan'; and se bisceop cwæð, 'Eala
þu leofa cyning, þin folc lið ofslagen and þu næfst þone
60 fultum þæt þu feohtan mæge, and þas flotmen cumað and
þe cucenne gebindað, butan þu mid fleame þinum feore
gebeorge, oððe þu þe swa gebeorge þæt þu buge to him.' Þa
cwæð Eadmund cyning swa swa he ful cene wæs, 'Þæs ic
gewilnige and gewisce mid mode, þæt ic ane ne belife æfter
65 minum leofum þegnum, þe on heora bedde wurdon, mid
bearnum and wifum, færlice ofslagene fram þysum flot-
mannum. Næs me næfre gewunelic þæt ic worhte fleames, ac
ic wolde swiðor sweltan gif ic þorfte for minum agenum
earde; and se ælmihtiga God wat þæt ic nelle abugan fram
70 his biggengum æfre, ne fram his soþan lufe, swelte ic, lybbe
ic.'
Æfter þysum wordum he gewende to þam ærendracan þe
Hingwar him to sende, and sæde him unforht, 'Witodlice þu
wære wyrðe sleges nu, ac ic nelle afylan on þinum fulum

56 synd] AOU; beoð B. 57 gefeohte] OU; feohte AB, in A ge inserted
by rev. 62 gebeorge (second)] A; gebeorghe O; beorge BU. 63 þæs]
AOU; þæs B. 64 ane] AB, in A altered to ana by rev.; ana OU. belife]
AOU; bileafe B. 65 bedde] A; beddum BOU. 70 swelte] AB, in A s
altered from w; swilte U. 73 him to] AU; to him B. Witodlice] A;
witodlice BOU. 74 wyrðe sleges nu] A; wyrðe nu sleges U (and O?);
nu weorðe slæges B. 74 f on þinum fulum blode mine clænan hande]
AU, in A hande altered to handa by rev.; mine clæne handæn on þine
fule blode BO.

64 ane: for ana, 'alone' (see I 193n); see Intro. p. 10, and cp textual
notes.
65 bedde: distributive sg. (but cp textual notes): 'OE sometimes
uses a singular noun in this way when the number of individual
possessors is plural, but each has only one of the things in question'
(Primer, VI 64n); cp 217 below, III 255, etc.
70 f swelte ic, lybbe ic: for the construction see QW § 159.
72 Æfter . . . 80 gebuge: from Abbo IX.
74 wære: probably pret.subj.: when the pret.subj. is used in OE in
expressions of propriety relating to present or future time, it is the
realization of the proper action which is in doubt, not, as might

blode mine clænan hande, for ðan þe ic Criste folgie, þe us 75
swa gebysnode; and ic bliðelice wille beon ofslagen þurh
eow, gif hit swa God foresceawað. Far nu swiþe hraðe and
sege þinum reþan hlaforde, "[N]e abihð næfre Eadmund
Hingware on life, hæþenum heretogan, buton he to Hælende
Criste ærest mid geleafan on þysum lande gebuge." '   80

þa gewende se ærendraca ardlice aweg and gemette be
wæge þone wælhreowan Hingwar mid eallre his fyrde, fuse
to Eadmunde, and sæde þam arleasan hu him geandwyrd
wæs. Hingwar þa bebead mid bylde þam sciphere þæt hi
þæs cynincges anes ealle cepan sceoldon, þe his hæse 85
forseah, and hine sona bindan. Hwæt þa Eadmund cynincg,
mid þam þe Hingwar com, stod innan his healle, þæs
Hælendes gemyndig, and awearp his wæpna: wolde
geæfenlæcan Cristes gebysnungum, þe forbead Petre mid
wæpnum to winnenne wið þa wælhreowan Iudeiscan. Hwæt 90
þa arleasan þa Eadmund gebundon and gebysmrodon
huxlice and beoton mid saglum, and swa syððan læddon
þone geleaffullan cyning to anum eorðfæstum treowe and
tigdon hine þærto mid heardum bendum, and hine eft

75 *criste folgige*] AU; *folgige criste* BO. 76 *and*] AU; *ac* B.
77 *swa*] AU; om. B; om. (or transposed?) O. *Far*] AOU; *fare* B.
78 *Ne*] *ne* ABU. 79 *hælende*] AB; *hælendum* OU. 81 *ardlice*] AU;
heardlice B. 83 *geandwyrd*] AOU; *iandswæred*] B. 84 *þa bebead*]
AOU; *bead þa* B. 85 *hæse*] A; *here* BU. 86 *Hwæt*] AOU; *hwæt* B.
87 *stod innan*] ABO; *stod ða innan* U. 90 *to winnenne*] AU (and O?);
to feohten B. 91 *þa arleasan þa*] AU (and O?); *þa þa arleasan* B. 91f
gebysmrodon huxlice] ABO; *huxlice gebysmorode* U.

appear, its propriety (see F. Behre, *The Subjunctive in OE Poetry*
(Göteborg, 1934) 55 f); cp also l. 210 below, and III 326.

74 *fulum:* dat.sg.neut.def. (wk.), see Intro. p. 11.

75 *hande:* acc.pl., see Intro. p. 10, and ·n textual notes.

81 *þa gewende . . . 107 Criste:* from Abbo X.

82 *wæge:* for *wege*, see Intro. p. 7. *fuse:* pl., referring to Hinguar and
his men (*Primer*, VI 80n).

85 *þæs cynincges anes:* 'only the king': see I 193n. *hæse:* Abbo
legibus (cp textual notes).

88 *wæpna:* neut.pl., see Intro. p. 10.

89 *geæfenlæcan:* for *-efen-*, see Intro. p. 7.

95 swungon langlice mid swipum; and he symble clypode
betwux þam swinglum mid soðan geleafan to Hælende
Criste; and þa hæþenan þa for his geleafan wurdon wodlice
yrre, for þan þe he clypode Crist him to fultume. Hi scuton
þa mid gafelucum, swilce him to gamenes, to, oð þæt he eall
100 wæs besæt mid heora scotungum, swilce igles byrsta, swa
swa Sebastianus wæs. Þa geseah Hingwar, se arlease flot-
man, þæt se æþela cyning nolde Criste wiðsacan, ac mid
anrædum geleafan hine æfre clypode: het hine þa beheaf-
dian, and þa hæðenan swa dydon. Betwux þam þe he cly-
105 pode to Criste þagit, þa tugon þa hæþenan þone halgan to
slæge and mid anum swencge slogon him of þæt heafod, and
his sawl siþode gesælig to Criste. Þær wæs sum man gehende
gehealden þurh God, behyd þam hæþenum, þe þis gehyrde
eall and hit eft sæde swa swa we [hit] secgað her.
110 Hwæt ða se flothere ferde eft to scipe and behyddon þæt
heafod þæs halgan Eadmundes on þam þiccum bremelum
þæt hit bebyrged ne wurde. Þa æfter fyrste, syððan hi

95 *swungon*] AU, in A altered to *swuncgon*, probably by rev.;
swuncgon B. 97 *wurdon*] AOU; *wurdon þa* B. *wodlice* AOU; *swyðe* B.
98 *Hi*] AU; *hi* OB. 99 *swilce him to gamenes to*] AU; *him togeanes* B.
102 *ac*] AU; *and* altered to *ac* (or vice versa) B. 103 *het*] ABO; *he het*
U. 107 *his*] AOU; om. B. *þær*] AU; *þær* BO. 109 *hit*] BOU; inserted
in A by rev. 112 *þa*] AOU; *þa* B.

96 *soðan*: dat.sg.m.indef. (strong), see Intro. p. 10.

98 *Hi scuton . . . 99 to*: they shot at him; *swilce him to gamenes*, as
if to amuse themselves: cp I 14n, and BT s.v. *to* II (5).

100 *besæt*: for *beset(t)*, p.pt., see Intro. p. 7.

101 *Sebastianus*: cp Ælfric's homily on St Sebastian, LS V 425 ff.
arlease: nom.sg.m.def.(wk.), see Intro. p. 10.

106 *slæge*: for *slege*, see Intro. p. 7.

106 *him*: possessive dat.: *him . . . þæt heafod*, 'his head'; so also at
III 105, 222, 223, 268 f; cp QW § 108, *Primer*, § 87(1).

107 *þær . . . 109 her*: from Abbo XII ll. 1–7.

110 *Hwæt ða . . . 112 wurde*: from Abbo XI. The Danish army left
E. Anglia in the autumn of 870. They returned four years later and
spent twelve months at Cambridge (874–5); they returned again in
879, this time to divide and settle the region (880). The Danish
kingdom of E. Anglia came to an end in 917.

112 *þa æfter . . . 121 heafod*: from Abbo XII l. 7–end.

afarenc wæron, com þæt landfolc to, þe þær to lafe wæs þa,
þær heora hlafordes lic læg butan heafde, and wurdon
swiðe sarige for his slege on mode, and huru þæt hi næfdon 115
þæt heafod to þam bodige. Þa sæde se sceawere þe hit ær
geseah, þæt þa flotmen hæfdon þæt heafod mid him, and
wæs him geðuht, swa swa hit wæs ful soð, þæt hi behyddon
þæt heafod on þam holte forhwega. Hi eodon þa ealle
endemes to þam wuda, secende gehwær, geond þyfelas and 120
bremelas, gif hi ahwær mihton gemeton þæt heafod.

Wæs eac micel wundor þæt an wulf wearð asend þurh
Godes wissunge to bewerigenne þæt heafod wið þa oþre deor
ofer dæg and niht. Hi eodon þa secende and symle cly-
pigende, swa swa hit gewunelic is þam ðe on wuda gað oft, 125
'[H]wær eart þu nu, gefera?', and him andwyrde þæt heafod,
'Her! [H]er! [H]er!', and swa gelome clypode, andswarigende
him eallum, swa oft swa heora ænig clypode, oþ þæt hi ealle
becomen þurh ða clypunga him to. Þa læg se græge wulf þe
bewiste þæt heafod, and mid his twam fotum hæfde þæt 130

113 *to*] ABO; om. U. *wæs þa*] A; *þa wæs* BOU. 114 *læg butan
heafde*] AU; *buton heafde l(æ)g* O; *buton heafde þa læg* B. 116 *þa*] AU;
þa B. 119 *Hi*] AU; *hi* OB. 119 *eodon þa* . . . 120 *secende*] UBO;
eodon þa secende . . . *secende* A. 119 f *ealle endemes*] AU; *endemes
ealle* OB. 121 *ahwær*] AU; om. B, and (probably) O. 122 *wearð*]
AU; *wæs* B. 123 *wissunge*] ABO; *mihte* U, glossed [*wi*]*ssunge* (the
first two letters cut away by binder) in margin in similar, if not
same, hand as text. 124 *and niht*] ABO; *and ofer niht* U. *Hi*] ABU;
hi O. *symle*] AOU; om. B. 125 *þam ðe*] AU; *þa ðe* O; *þæt ða þe* B.
126 *Hwær*] U; *hwær* AB. *gefera*] AOU; *gerefa* B. *and*] ABO; *And*
U. *andwyrde*] AOU; *andswyrde* B. 127 *Her* (second & third)] BU;
her A. 128 *him* . . . *clypode*] AOU; om. B. 129 *græge*] A, altered to
græga by rev.; *græga* OU; *grægæ* B.

119 f *ealle endemes:* for the word-order (cp textual notes) cp III 195.
121 *gemeton:* inf., see Intro. p. 10.
122 *Wæs eac* . . . 124 *niht:* Abbo XIII ll. 16–23: the departure
from Abbo's arrangement seems curiously inept.
124 *Hi eodon* . . . 129 *him to:* from Abbo XIII ll. 1–16.
129 *becomen:* pret.pl., see Intro. p. 10. *clypunga:* probably for
clypunge (as in OU), acc.sg; see Intro. p. 10.
129 *þa læg* . . . 133 *hyrdrædenne:* from Abbo XIII l. 23–end.
129 *græge:* nom.sg.m.def.(wk.), see Intro. p. 10, and cp textual
notes.

heafod beclypped, grædig and hungrig, and for Gode ne
dorste þæs heafdes abyrian, [ac] heold hit wið deor. þa
wurdon hi ofwundrode þæs wulfes hyrdrædenne, and þæt
halige heafod ham feredon mid him, þancigende þam
135 Ælmihtigan ealra his wundra; ac se wulf folgode forð mid
þam heafde, oþ þæt hi to tune comon, swylce he tam wære,
and gewende eft siþþan to wuda ongean. þa landleoda þa
siþþan ledon þæt heafod to þam halgan bodige and bebyrig-
don hine swa swa hi selost mihton on swylcere hrædinge,
140 and cyrcan arærdan sona him onuppon.

132 *ac*] BU; *and* A. *þa*] AU; *þa* BO. 139 *hine*] AU; om. B; om. (or
transposed) O. *swa swa*] ABO; *swa. swa swa* U. *selost*] AU; *leohtlicost*
OB. *mihton on*] ABU; two or three letters illegible before *on* in O.
140 *arærdan*] A, second *r* altered (from *w*?); *arærdon* BOU. *sona*]
AU; om. B; om. (or transposed) O. *him onuppon*] AOU; *onuppon*
him B.

133 *and þæt* . . . 140 *onuppon*: from Abbo XIV ll. 1–15.
138 f *and bebyrigdon hine*: according to a tradition which goes back
to the beginning of the twelfth century, Edmund met his death and
was buried at Hoxne in Suffolk. This cannot, however, be reconciled
with the accounts given by Abbo, and Hermann, monk of Bury, in
his *Liber de Miraculis Sancti Eadmundi* (*c.* 1100). According to Abbo
Edmund was staying at the time of the viking invasion, *in villa quæ
lingua eorum Hægelisdun dicitur, a qua et silva vicina eodem nomine
vocatur* (VI ll. 13 f). It was there that he died, and his burial seems
from Abbo's account to have been in or near the same place.
Hægelisdun cannot be identified with Hoxne: it is probably Helles-
don, near Norwich (see EHR xl (1925) 223, fn. 3). According to
Hermann, Edmund was buried, *ut majorum nobis intimarunt relata,
in villula Suthtune dicta, de prope loco martyrizationis.* There are a
number of Suttons in E. Anglia, but none of them is near Hoxne.
There is one in Wymondham a few miles from Hellesdon (EHR,
loc.cit.); it has also been suggested that it is Sutton Hoo, the burial
place of the kings of E. Anglia, that is referred to (R. Rainbird
Clarke, *East Anglia* (1960), 156). The church at Hoxne, dedicated
to Æthelberht, an earlier martyr king of E. Anglia (d. 794), was the
cathedral for Suffolk during the century preceding the Norman Con-
quest. I do not think the omission in BO at l. 144 is deliberate, but if
it were, whoever made it, apparently identified the earlier place of
burial with Bury St Edmunds (see 141–7n).
139 *swa swa hi selost mihton*: ' "as best they could", "as well as
they could". This construction, with superlative adverb next the

Eft þa on fyrste, æfter fela gearum, þa seo hergung geswac and sibb wearð forgifen þam geswenctan folce, þa fengon hi togædere and worhton ane cyrcan wurðlice þam halgan, for þan ðe gelome wundra wurdon æt his byrgene æt þam gebædhuse þær he bebyrged wæs. Hi woldon þa ferian 145 mid folclicum wurðmynte þone halgan lichaman and læcgan innan þære cyrcan; þa wæs micel wundor þæt he wæs eallswa gehal swilce he cucu wære, mid clænum lichaman, and his swura wæs gehalod, þe ær wæs forslagen, and wæs swylce an seolcen þræd embe his swuran ræd, mannum to 150 swutelunge hu he ofslagen wæs. Eac swilce þa wunda þe þa wælhreowan hæþenan mid gelomum scotungum on his lice macodon, wæron gehælede þurh þone heofonlican God; and he lið swa ansund oþ þisne andwerdan dæg, andbidende æristes and þæs ecan wuldres. His lichama us cyð, þe lið 155

144 *for þan ðe . . . wurdon*] AU; om. BO. 148 *eallswa*] A; *eall* BU. 149 *wæs forslagen*] A; *forslagen wæs* BOU. 150 *ræd*] A, *æ* altered from another letter (?); *read* OU; om. B. 151 *þa wunda*] AU; *wundræ* (om. *þa*) B. 154 *andbidigende*] AU; *abidende* B.

---

verb, is the normal way of expressing such a qualification' (*Primer*, VI 137n; cp Ericson, *The Use of Swa in OE* (Göttingen, 1932) ch. IX); cp also III 301.

140 *cyrcan:* referred to below l. 145 as *þam gebædhuse.* It was, according to Abbo, a very humble building (XIV ll. 15, 23). *aværdan:* pret.pl., see Intro. p. 10.

141 *Eft þa . . . 147 cyrcan:* from Abbo XIV l. 16 to end. The new church was built, in Abbo's words, *in villa regia quæ lingua Anglorum Bedricesgueord dicitur* (XIV ll. 26 f). *Bedricesgueord* (OE *Bedricesweorð*) is the modern Bury St Edmunds. The date of the translation is not known: Ælfric follows Abbo in saying merely, that it was many years after the first interment. Later writers date it variously between 903 and 939 (see Arnold, R.S. 96 (1890) vol. i, p. xxi, and cp EHR xl (1925) 223, fn. 2). It was certainly before 945, when a grant of land was made to the monastery by Edmund, King of Wessex (KCD ii 258; Arnold, *op.cit.*, 340 ff).

145 *gebædhuse:* for -*bed*-, see Intro. p. 7.
146 f *læcgan:* for *lecgan,* see Intro. p. 7.
147 *þa wæs . . . 155 wuldres:* from Abbo XV ll. 1–11.
150 *ræd:* for *read;* cp textual notes, and see SB § 76 Anm.
155 *His lichama . . . 157 siþode:* from Abbo XIX ll. 1–18.

unformolsnod, þæt he butan forligre her on worulde leofode
and mid clænum life to Criste siþode. Sum wudewe wunode,
Oswyn gehaten, æt þæs halgan byrgene on gebedum and
fæstenum manega gear syððan; seo wolde efsian ælce geare
160 þone sanct and his næglas ceorfan syferlice mid lufe and on
scryne healdan to haligdome on weofode.

Þa wurðode þæt landfolc mid geleafan þone sanct, and
Þeodred bisceop þearle mid gifum on golde and on seolfre
[gegodode þæt mynster] þam sancte to wurðmynte. Þa
165 comon on sumne sæl ungesælige þeofas, eahte on anre nihte,

158 æt . . . byrgene] AOU; om. B. 162 þa] AU; þa B. 162 and . . .
163 seolfre] AU; om. B. 164 gegodode þæt mynster] U; om. AB. þam
sancte] AU; om. B. 165 þeofas] AU; þeowæs B. eahte] A, altered to
eahta by rev.; eahta BU.

---

157 Sum wudewe . . . 161 weofode: from Abbo XV ll. 13–23.

162 þa wurðode . . . 191 sceolde: from Abbo XVI.

163 þeodred bisceop . . . 164 wurðmynte: Abbo does not specifically
mention Theodred as a benefactor. It is not certain which of various
bishops named Theodred is referred to. Abbo says, beatæ memoriæ
Theodredus, ejusdem provinciæ religiosus episcopus, qui propter
meritorum prærogativam bonus appellabatur, but says nothing that
would help to identify him more precisely. Two of the bishops of
Elmham between the restoration of the see c. 950 and the end of the
tenth century, bore the name Theodred: the first of them was con-
secrated between 964 and 975, the second was bishop from between
975 and 982, until 995: one of them was a generous benefactor of
St Edmunds (see EHR xl (1925) 224, fn. 2). Before 951 Suffolk at least
seems to have been under the jurisdiction of the bishop of London,
whose name was also Theodred, and who was also a benefactor of the
monastery (see D. Whitelock, Anglo-Saxon Wills (1930) p. 4. ll. 3–6).
Abbo's words may imply that Theodred was dead at the time he
(Abbo) was writing (but see Arnold's note ad.loc.): if so, it would be
either Theodred of London, or Theodred I of Elmham, to whom the
story refers. William of Malmesbury identifies him with the former;
and in view of the episode related here, it is of interest to note that
'it was by Theodred [of London] that King Athelstan sent word to
the archbishop that he considered the laws against young thieves too
severe (VI Ath.12.1)' (Whitelock, op.cit., p. 99). On the ecclesiastical
history of E. Anglia at this date, see D. Whitelock, 'The Conversion
of the Eastern Danelaw', Saga-Book of the Viking Society xii (1937–
45) 171 f.

165 eahte: for eahta, see Intro. p. 10, and cp textual notes.

to þam arwurðan halgan: woldon stelan þa maðmas þe men
þyder brohton, and cunnodon mid cræfte hu hi in cumon
mihton. Sum sloh mid slecge swiðe þa hæpsan, sum heora
mid feolan feolode abutan, sum eac underdealf þa duru mid
spade, sum heora mid hlæddre wolde unlucan þæt ægðyrl: 170
[a]c hi swuncon on idel and earmlice ferdon, swa þæt se
halga wer hi wundorlice geband, ælcne swa he stod struti-
gende mid tole, þæt heora nan ne mihte þæt morð gefrem-
man, ne hi þanon astyrian, ac stodon swa oð mergen. Men
þa þæs wundrodon hu þa weargas hangodon, sum [upp]on 175
hlæddre, sum leat to gedelfe, and ælc on his weorce wæs
fæste gebunden. Hi wurdon þa gebrohte to þam bisceope
ealle and he het hi hon on heagum gealgum ealle; [a]c he
næs na gemyndig hu se mildheorta God clypode þurh his
witegan þas word þe her standað: [e]os qui ducuntur ad 180
mortem eruere ne cesses ([þ]a þe man læt to deaðe, alys hi ut
symble); and eac þa halgan canones gehadodum forbeodað,
ge bisceopum, ge preostum, to beonne embe þeofas, for þan
þe hit ne gebyrað þam þe beoð gecorene Gode to þegnigenne,

166 *woldon*] AU; *and wolden* B. 169 *feolode*] AU; *feoledon* B. 170
wolde] A; *woldon* UB. 171 *ac*] B; *Ac* AU. 173 *þæt* (first)]ABO, in A
æ altered from *e. nan*] ABU, in A inserted by original scribe. 174
stodon] AU; *heo stodon* B. 175 *uppon*] BU; *on* A. 178 *ealle* (second)]
AB; om. U. *ac*] B; *Ac* AU. 180 *eos*] *Eos* ABU. 181 *þa*] *Þa* ABU. *hi*]
AU; om. B. 182 *and*] AB; *And* U.

167 *cumon*: inf., see Intro. p. 10.

170 *ægðyrl*: for *eagðyrl*, see SB §§ 76 Anm., 121.

172 *strutigende*: *strutian* is not otherwise recorded in OE, and the
meaning is uncertain. Abbo has, *Sicque disposito opere, cum singuli
certatim insudant pro virium facultate, sanctus martyr eos ligat in ipso
conamine.* For the senses of the word in Middle, and later English,
and of cognate forms, see NED s.v. *strut*, vb.[1]

174 *stodon*: on the ungrammatical plural see I 159n.

175 *uppon*: the reading of BU, which seems rhythmically prefer-
able.

180 *eos* . . . 181 *cesses*: Proverbs 24[11], as quoted by Abbo.

181 *hi*: the reading of B is at first sight attractive, but cp LS
XXIV 116 f, where a similar Latin construction is translated in the
same way.

182 *þa halgan canones* . . . 186 *penas*: cp HB 3:80 ff.

185 þæt hi geþwærlæcan sceolon on æniges mannes deaðe, gif
hi beoð Drihtnes þenas. Eft þa Ðeodred bisceop sceawode
his bec syððan: behreowsode mid geomerunge þæt he swa
reðne dom sette þam ungesæligum þeofum, and hit besar-
gode æfre, oð his lifes ende, and þa leode bæd georne þæt hi
190 him mid fæstan fullice þry dagas, biddende þone Ælmihtigan
þæt he him arian sceolde.

On þam lande wæs sum man, Leofstan gehaten, rice for
worulde and unwittig for Gode, se rad to þam halgan mid
riccetere swiðe and het him æteowian orhlice swiðe þone
195 halgan sanct, hwæþær he gesund wære; ac swa hraðe swa he
geseah þæs sanctes lichaman, þa awedde he sona and wæl-
hreowlice grymete[de] and earmlice geendode yfelum deaðe.

---

186 *Eft þa*] AU; *Eft þa ða* B. 186 f *sceawode his bec syððan*] A;
syððan he his bec sceawode BU. 187 *behreowsode*] AU; *bereowsode*
or, possibly, *he reowsode* B. 190 *him mid*] AB; *mid him* U. *þone*
ælmihtigan] A; om. *þone* U; *þone ælmihtigæn god* B. 193 *and*] AU;
om. B. *unwittig*] AB; *ungewittig* U. 197 *grymetede*] AB, in A altered
from *grymete* by rev.; *grymytte* U.

---

186 *Eft þa* . . . 187 *behreowsode:* for the construction see I 39n.
The reading of BU may be original (parallel instances of subordinate
clauses with *siððan* interrupting the main clause occur, e.g. LS
XXVIII 24 ff), but it has more the appearance of a copyist's treat-
ment of an unfamiliar idiom, and it is not easy to see how, if it were
original, the reading of A could have arisen; see Intro. p. 5, fn. 4.

190 *fæstan:* pret.subj.pl., see Intro. p. 10.

192 *On þam lande* . . . 197 *deaðe:* from Abbo XVII.

192 *Leofstan:* Abbo says his father's name was Ælfgar: the name is
not uncommon, and it may be no more than a coincidence that the
Ealdorman Ælfgar (died after 951), father-in-law of Edmund, King
of Wessex, was an East Anglian.

194 *æteowian* . . . 195 *wære:* on this construction, in which the
noun subject of the dependent noun clause is anticipated and made
object of the main clause, see MP iii (1905–6) 253 f. Translate 'show
him . . . whether the holy saint was uncorrupted'; cp also III 3 f.

194 *orhlice:* see Intro. p. 11; on *h* < *g* see Campbell § 446.

197 *grymetede:* 3 sg.pret.ind. of *grymetian*, cons.(wk.) vb. (2): this
is the form of the pret. elsewhere in LS (XI 62, XXV 540, VI 197).
The original reading of A (if not an error) may be for *grymette* (cp U),
3 sg.pret.ind. of *grymettan*, cons.(wk.) vb. (1); see Intro. p. 9.

Þis is ðam gelic þe se geleaffulla papa Gregorius sæde on his
gesetnysse be ðam halgan Laurentię, ðe lið on Romebyrig—
þæt menn woldon sceawian symle hu he lage, ge gode, ge 200
yfele; ac God hi gestilde, swa þæt þær swulton on þære
sceawunge ane seofon menn ætgædere: þa geswicon þa oþre
to sceawigenne þone martyr mid menniscum gedwylde.

Fela wundra we gehyrdon on folclicre spræce be þam
halgan Eadmunde, þe we her nellað on gewrite settan; ac hi 205
wat gehwa. On þysum halgan is swutel, and on swilcum
oþrum, þæt God ælmihtig mæg þone man aræran eft on
domes dæg andsundne of eorþan, se þe hylt Eadmunde
halne his lichaman oð þone micclan dæg, þeah ðe he of
moldan come. Wyrðe [wære] seo stow for þam wurðfullan 210
halgan þæt hi man wurþ[ode] and wel gelog[ode] mid
clænum Godes þeowum to Cristes þeowdome, for þan þe se
halga is mærra þonne men magon asmeagan.

198 þe se] AU; þe B. geleaffulla] AU; halga B. sæde] AU; om. B.
200 symle] AU; om. B. 200 f ge gode ge yfele] AU; om. B. 201 swulton]
ABU, in A l altered from r. 204 Fela] AU; felæ B. 207 eft] ABU;
om. (or transposed) V. 209 his] AUV; om. B. of] AU; on B. 210
Wyrðe] AUV; weorðe B. wære] BU, and (probably) V; in A four or
five letters erased after Wyrðe, and is inserted by rev. 211 wurþode]
wurðode UV; wæl wurðode B; wurþige A, ige by rev. on erasure. wel
gelogode] UV; wælegode B; wel gelogige A, ige by rev. on erasure.

198 Þis . . . 202 ætgædere: from Abbo XVIII ll. 1–6. Gregorius:
Gregory the Great, pope from 590 to 604; the incident is related in
one of his letters (Lib. IV, Epist. XXX (Pat. Lat. lxxvii 701 f)).

202 þa . . . 203 gedwylde: not in Abbo.

204 Fela . . . 206 gehwa: cp Abbo XVIII ll. 11–14.

206 On þysum . . . 210 come: not in Abbo.

208 Eadmunde: 'for Edmund', dat. of advantage; cp III 132n, and
Primer, § 87(1).

210 Wyrðe . . . 211 wurþode: Abbo XVIII ll. 6 f; on the use of the
subjunctive see above l. 74n.

211 wel gelogode . . . 212 þeowdome: cp Abbo XIX ll. 18–26, where
Abbo exhorts those in whose keeping the shrine then was, to greater
purity of life. At that time the church was served by a small com-
munity of clerks (cp III 22, 24n). The alterations in A were clearly
made after 1020 when the clerks were dispossessed and Benedictines
installed in their place (see RES NS ix (1958) 160 f).

Nis Angelcynn bedæled Drihtnes halgena, þonne on Engla
215 landa licgað swilce halgan swylce þæs halga cyning, and
Cuþberht se eadiga, and Æþeldryð on Elig, and eac hire
swustor, ansunde on lichaman, geleafan to trymminge.
Synd eac fela oðre on Angelcynne halgan þe fela wundra
wyrcað—swa swa hit wide is cuð—þam Ælmihtigan to lofe,
220 þe hi on gelyfdon. Crist geswutelað mannum þurh his
mæran halgan þæt he is Ælmihtig God þe macað swilce wun-
dra, þeah þe þa earman Iudei hine eallunga wiðsocen, for

214 *angelcynn*] AUV; *angol* B. *þonne*] AU; *forþam* B. 215 *is*
inserted after *cyning* by rev. in A; om. BU. 216 *sancte* inserted
before *æþeldryð* by rev. in A; om. BUV. *elig*] ABUV, in A *e* altered
from *h*. 217 *ansunde*] ABU; *ealle andsunde* V. 218 *Synd*] AU;
Beoð B. *halgan*] AUV; om. B. 219 *is cuð*] ABV; *cuð is* U. 220
Crist] AUV; *Crist sylf* B. 222 *þeah þe*] ABU; *þeah* V. *iudei*] AU;
Iudeiscæn B.

---

214 *Nis . . . 220 gelyfdon:* not in Abbo, but the sentence in Abbo
on which ll. 210 f are based, continues (*locus . . .*) *in quo tantæ
virtutes fiunt et factæ esse referuntur, quantas hac tempestate apud
Anglos nusquam alibi audivimus* (XVIII ll. 8–10); and Ælfric pos-
sibly wished to correct something that might well have appeared to
him to give a wrong impression.

215 *landa:* dat.sg., see Intro. p. 10.

215 *þæs:* for *þes* nom.sg.m., see Intro. p. 7.

216 *Cuþberht se eadiga:* see I 229–32n.

216 *Æþeldryð . . . 217 swustor:* the story of St Audrey and her sister
Sexburh is told by Bede HE iv 17 (on which is based Ælfric's Life,
LS XX). *sancte* (textual notes): Ælfric in LS, and the reviser of
MS A, use either *sancta* or *sancte* (without article) before feminine
proper names, apparently without distinction of case (see, e.g., LS
III 237, 242, VII 420, XXV 519 (rev.)); cp I 144n.

217 *lichaman:* distributive sg., see above l. 65n.

220 *Crist . . . 229 Gaste:* not in Abbo.

222 *wiðsocen:* pret.pl., see Intro. p. 10.

222 *for þan þe:* 'because'; although this is the reading of all
MSS (ABU, *for ðon ðe* V), *for þan*, 'therefore', would give better
sense.

þan þe hi synd awyrgede, swa swa hi wiscton him sylfum. Ne beoð nane wundra geworhte æt heora byrgenum, for ðan þe hi ne gelyfað on þone lifigendan Crist; ac Crist ge- 225 swutelað mannum hwær se soða geleafa is, þonne he swylce wundra wyrcð þurh his halgan wide geond þas eorðan. þæs him sy wuldor a mid his heofonlican Fæder and þam Halgan Gaste. Amen.

223 *synd*] AUV; *beoð* B. 226 *soða*] AUV; *gode* B. 227 f *þæs him sy*] AUV; *þam beo* B. 228 *wuldor*] AU; *wuldor and lof* BV. *halgan gaste. AMEN*] UV; *halgan gaste a b[uton ende . . .] AMEN* B, erased but partly legible; *a buton ende* inserted after *gaste* by rev. in A.

223 *swa swa . . . sylfum:* the reference is to Mat. 27[25] (cp CH II 252 f/31 ff and 256/19 ff). Ælfric refers frequently to the punishment of the Jews for their rejection of Christ, and for their part in the Crucifixion (e.g. CH I 402; *Treatise on the Old and New Testaments* (ed. Crawford) ll. 1227–56; Assmann IV 239–48, V 67–95, VI 179–85); cp also III 364 ff note.

III

ST SWITHIN, BISHOP

On Eadgares dagum ðæs æðelan cynincges, þa ða se
cristendom wæs wel ðeonde þurh God on Angelcynne under
ðam ylcan cynincge, þa geswutelode God þone sanct
Swyðun mid manegum wundrum, þæt he mære is. His
5 dæda næron cuðe ær ðan þe hi God sylf cydde, ne we ne
fundon on bocum hu se bisceop leofode on þysre worulde
ær ðan þe he gewende to Criste. Þæt wæs þære gymeleast
þe on life hine cuþon, þæt hi noldon awritan his weorc and
drohtnunge þam towerdum mannum ðe his mihte ne
10 cuðon; ac God hæfð swaþeah his lif geswutelod mid swute-
lum wundrum and syllicum tacnum. Ðes Swyðun wæs
bisceop on Winceastre, swaþeah ofer Hamtunscire gesælig

7 þære] A, altered to þæra by rev.   11 Ðes] A, e altered from æ.

1–11 *tacnum:* are very similar to *Epitome* § 1; for ll. 1–4 *is,* cp
Landferth, *Prologus* (i 4), and for 5 *ne we* . . . 11 *tacnum,* cp Land-
ferth, *Epistola* (i 1).

1 *On Eadgares dagum:* Edgar ruled jointly with his brother Edwy
from 957 till Edwy's death in 959; he was sole king from then until
his own death in 975; see also below ll. 369–86n and 371–2n.

3 *geswutelode* . . . 4 *is:* for the construction see II 194–5n.

3 f *sanct Swyðun:* all we can add with any certainty to the in-
formation given here, are the dates of his episcopate, which began in
852, and lasted till his death in 862. His burial was commemorated
on July 2, the day for which Ælfric's homily was written (but only O
(as recorded by Wanley) has the correct rubric *Depositio (Natale* A)
Sancti Suuithuni mitissimi Episcopi; see also I 122–3n). July 15, the
present St Swithin's day, commemorates his translation (see below ll.
18–19n).

7 *þære:* gen.pl., see Intro. p. 10, and cp textual notes.

11 *Ðes Swyðun* . . . 14 *Aðelwolde:* not in Landferth, or *Epitome.*

12 *ofer Hamtunscire:* in Ælfric's time only Hampshire and Surrey
came under the jurisdiction of the bishop of Winchester, but in
Swithin's day the diocese also included Wiltshire and Berkshire: the
diocese was divided in 910.

Godes þeowa, and eahte bisceopas wæron betwux him and
Aðelwolde. [N]u næs us his lif cuð, swa swa we ær cwædon,
butan þæt he wæs bebyrged æt his bisceopstole bewestan 15
þære cyrcan and oferworht syððan, oþ þæt his wundra
geswutelodon his gesælða mid Gode.

Þrym gearum ær ðan þe [se] sanct into cyrcan wære
gebroht of ðære stænenan þryh þe stent nu wiðinnan þam
niwan geweorce, com se arwurða Swyðun to sumum ge- 20
lyfedan smyðe on swefne æteowiende wurðlice geglencged,
and ðas word him cwæð to, 'Canst þu ðone preost þe is

---

13 *eahte*] A, altered to *eahta* by rev. 14 *sancte* inserted before *aðel-
wolde* in A by rev. *Nu*] *nu* A. 17 *geswutelodon*] AO; *swutelodon* G.
18 *se*] AGO, in A inserted by rev. 19 *of*] AG; *on* O.

---

13 *eahte:* for *eahta*, cp Intro. p. 10, and cp textual notes.

14 *Aðelwolde:* bishop of Winchester 963–84, one of the leaders
of the Benedictine revival in England; see J. Armitage Robinson,
The Times of St Dunstan (1923) ch. V. Ælfric himself was a pupil
of Athelwold's at Winchester (see Intro. pp. 14 f, and cp ll. 217 ff
below).

15 *he wæs* . . . 17 *Gode:* there is a brief reference to the place of
Swithin's burial in Landferth, *Prologus* (i 4) (inserted by a later hand
in the Rouen MS, but incorporated in the text in the Royal MS). It
is described at length, and his humility in choosing to be buried there,
at the end of c. II (i 16).

15 *his bisceopstole:* the Old Minster, Winchester, on which see
I 118n and below ll. 116–17n.

18 *þrym* . . . 78 *Hælend is:* cp Landferth I (i 5–9); *Epitome* §§ 2–5.

18 *þrym* . . . 19 *gebroht:* the remains of St Swithin were removed
into the cathedral July 15 971.

19 *of ðære* . . . 20 *geweorce:* not in Landferth, or *Epitome*; *þam
niwan geweorce:* Athelwold rebuilt the Old Minster; the new building
was dedicated on October 20 980.

20 f *gelyfedan:* dat.sg.m.indef. (strong), see Intro. p. 10. An adj.
following *sum* normally has the indef.decl., see e.g., below ll. 79,
291 f, and I 43 f; cp Schrader § 44.

22, 24 *preost:* in general, as at I 199, II 183, etc, a clerk in holy
orders (not necessarily, of course, priest's orders, i.e. not necessarily
a *mæssepreost:* for the seven ecclesiastical orders see HB I 29 ff,
2:115 ff, II 95 ff); in particular, as here, and frequently elsewhere in
OE, one of the clergy serving a non-monastic *mynster* (*preostlif:* see

gehaten Eadzige, þe wæs of Ealdan Mynstre mid ðam oðrum
preostum adræfed for heora unþeawum þurh Aðelwold bi-
25 sceop?' Se smið þa andwyrde þam arwurðan Swyðune þus,
'Gefyrn [i]c hine cuðe, leof; ac he ferde heonon and ic nat
to gewissan hwær he wunað nu.' Þa cwæð eft se halga wer
to ðam ealdan smyðe, 'Witodlice he wunað nu on Wincel-
cumbe hamfæst, and ic ðe nu halsige on þæs Hælendes
30 naman þæt ðu him min ærende ardlice abeode, and sege
him to soþan þæt Swiðun se bisceop het þæt he fare to
Aþelwolde bisceope and secge þæt he geopenige him sylf

---

24 þurh] AG, in A h inserted by original scribe. 26 ic] GO; Ic A.
31 to (second)] AGO, in A inserted above the line.

I 91–2n), as distinct from the *munecas* of a monastic *mynster* (*munuc-
lif*); female religious corresponding to *preostas* and *munecas* were
called *nunnan* and *mynecena* respectively. The Latin terms corre-
sponding to *preost* in the sense in which it is used in the present
passage are *canonicus* (the word which Landferth uses at this point),
and *clericus*, which were also borrowed into OE, as *canonic* and *cleric*
(see J. Armitage Robinson, *op.cit.*, 170 f). On the *ordo canonicus* in
western Europe in the early Middle Ages see J. C. Dickinson, *The
Origins of the Austin Canons and their Introduction into England*
(1950) 7–25.

23 þe wæs . . . 24 bisceop: the year following his appointment to
the see of Winchester, Athelwold, with the king's support, expelled
the clerks then in possession of the cathedral, and substituted monks
from Abingdon where he had previously been abbot. Soon after he
carried out the same process at the New Minster, Winchester, at
Milton Abbas, and at Chertsey (Chron. s.a. 964). In his life of Athel-
wold Ælfric gives an account of the expulsion of the clerks from the
cathedral and describes them as 'evil-living . . . possessed by pride,
insolence, and wanton behaviour, to such an extent that several of
them scorned to celebrate mass in their turn; they repudiated wives
whom they had married unlawfully, and took others; and were con-
tinually given over to gluttony and drunkenness' (trans. Dorothy
Whitelock, *English Historical Documents c. 500–1042* (1955) 835); see
also Plummer ii 157, and Thomas Symons, *Regularis Concordia* (1953)
xxii and fnn. 2, 3).

31 het: for hæt(t), 3 sg.pres.ind., although all three MSS have het;
see Intro. p. 7, and cp II 45n.

32 him sylf: sylf in OE is an adj. which emphasizes the noun or
pron. with which it agrees. It is normally used alone, but is sometimes

mine byrgene and mine ban gebringe binnan ðære cyrcan;
for ðan þe him is getiþod þæt ic on his timan beo man-
num geswutelod'; [a]nd se smið him cwæð to, 'La leof, 35
Eadzige nele gelyfan minum wordum.' Ða cwæð se bisceop
eft, 'Gange him to minre byrgene and ateo ane hringan up
of ðære þryh, and gif seo hringe him folgað æt þam forman
tige, þonne wat he to soðan þæt ic þe sende to him. Gif
seo hringe nele up þurh his anes tige, þonne ne sceall he 40
nateshwon þinre sage gelyfan. Sege him eac siððan þæt he
sylf gerihtlæce his dæda and þeawas to his Drihtnes willan,
and efste anmodlice to þam ecan life. Sege eac eallum
mannum þæt sona swa hi geopeniað mine byrgene, þæt hi
magon ðær findan swa deorwurðne hord þæt heora dyre 45
gold ne bið nahte wurð wið þa foresædan maðmas.'
    Se halga Swyðun þa ferde fram þam smiðe up and se
smið ne dorste secgan þas gesihðe ænigum menn: nolde
beon gesewen unsoðsagul boda. Hwæt ða se halga wer hine

---

34 *on*] AGO, in G inserted above the line, probably by original
scribe. 35 *and*] GO; *And* A. 36 *eadzige nele*] AO; *nele he* G. 37 *Gange
him*] AO; *Gange he* G. 38 *and*] AG; om. O. 45 *gold* inserted before
hord in A by rev.; om. G.

---

preceded by a pleonastic reflex.dat.pron.: so here, where *sylf* agrees
with the subject *he*, and the sense is 'he himself', 'he and no other';
cp also LS XXIV 102, *Þa awrat se Hælend him sylf þis gewrit* (for
further examples see Schrader § 95). This construction should be
distinguished from that in which the pron. is a reflex.dat. object, or
dat. of interest, when *sylf* agrees with it, as at l. 257 below and II 223.

34 *for ðan þe* . . . 35 *geswutelod:* there is nothing corresponding to
this clause in Sauv..ge's edition of Landferth, but the Royal MS and
Epitome have *quoniam quidem cęlitus illi est concessum, quod tempore
suo manifestandus sum.*

37 *Gange him:* a pleonastic reflex.dat.pron. is often used in OE
with vbs. of motion; cp also ll. 84, 160, 172, 330 below, and *Primer*
§ 87(1).

40 *his anes:* 'of him alone, his unaided'; cp I 193n.

45 *swa* . . . 46 *maðmas:* i.e. St Swithin's remains, as Landferth
explains (III (i 24)).

50 eft gespræc, and git þryddan siðe, and swyðe hine þreade
hwi he nolde gehyrsumian his hæsum mid weorce. Se smið
þa æt nextan eode to his byrgene, and genam ane hringan—
earhlice swaðeah—and clypode to Gode, þus cwæðende mid
wordum, 'Eala ðu Drihten God, ealra gesceafta scyppend,
55 getiða me synfullum þæt ic ateo þas hringan up of ðysum
hlyde gif se lið her on innan se ðe me spræc to on swæfne
þriwa.' He teah ða þæt isen up swa eaðelice of ðam stane
swilce hit on sande stode, and he swyðe þæs wundrode. He
ða hit eft sette on þæt ylce þyrl, and þyde mid his fet, and
60 hit swa fæste eft stod þæt nan man ne mihte hit þanon
ateon.

Þa eode se smið geegsod þanon and gemette on cypincge
þæs Eadzies mann and sæde him gewislice hwæt Swyðun
him bebead and bæd hine georne þæt he hit abude him. He
65 cwæð þæt he hit wolde cyðan his hlaforde and ne dorste
swaðeah hit secgan æt fruman, ær þan ðe he beþohte þæt
him ðearflic nære þæt he ðæs halgan hæse forhule his
hlaforde: sæde þa be endebyrdnysse hwæt Swyðun him
bebead. [þ]a onscunode se Eadsige Aðelwold þone bisceop
70 and ealle ða munecas þe on ðam mynstre wæron, for þære

---

51 weorce] AGO, in A final -e by original scribe on erasure of two
letters. 52 eode] GO; eode swaðeah A. 56 me spræc to] AO; spræc to
me G, me inserted by later hand. 57 up swa eaðelice] GO; up swa
eaðelice up A. 65 he hit wolde] A; he wolde hit GO. 67 forhule] A;
forhæle GO. 69 þa] þa AGO. aðelwold] AGO, in A followed by
erasure of one letter. bisceop] AG, in A followed by erasure of one
letter; ð O. 70 þære] A; þam GO.

---

53 cwæðende: for cweðende, see Intro. p. 7.

56 swæfne: for swefne, see Intro. p. 7.

67 forhule: 3 sg.pret.subj. of forhelan, perhaps influenced by vbs. of
class (3) strong with stems ending in l + cons., e.g. helpan. The
regular form is forhæle as in GO.

68 him: i.e. Eadsige.

69 þa onscunode . . . 71 wið hi: in his life of Athelwold Ælfric gives
an account (ch. 15) of an attempt by the dispossessed clerks to poison
Athelwold.

utdræfe þe he gedyde wið hi, and nolde gehyran þæs halgan
bebod, þeah ðe se sanct wære gesib him for worulde. He
gebeah swaþeah binnan twam gearum to þam ylcan
mynstre and munuc wearð þurh God and þær wunode oð
þæt he gewat of life. Geblætsod is se Ealmihtiga þe 75
geeadmed [þa] modigan and ða eadmodan ahæfð to heali-
cum geðincþum, and gerihtlæcð þa synfullan, and symle
hylt ða godan þe on hine hihtað, for ðan þe he Hælend is.

Eft wæs sum earm ceorl egeslice gehoferod and ðearle
gebiged þurh ðone bradan hofor; þam wearð geswutelod on 80
swefne gewislice þæt he sceolde gefeccan æt Swyðunes
byrgene his lichaman hæle and þære alefednysse. He aras ða
on mergen micclum fægnigende and mid twam criccum
creap him to Wynceastre and gesohte ðone sanct swa swa
him gesæd wæs, biddende his hæle gebigdum cneowum. He 85

75 *god* inserted after *ealmihtiga* in A by rev.; om. GO. 76 *þa*] GO;
þone A. 78 *hihtað*] A; *gehihtað* G, *ge* inserted by later hand. 85 *He*]
AG; *he* O.

70 f *þære utdræfe:* on the variable gender of some *i*-stem nouns (cp
textual notes), see Campbell §§ 606, 609 f. This is the only recorded
occurrence of the word; the simplex is fem.

72 *þeah ðe . . . worulde:* not in Landferth; it is not clear whether
se sanct refers to Swithin or Athelwold, whose sanctity was recog-
nized in 996, when his remains were translated into the choir of
Winchester cathedral; see Sisam, *Studies,* 171 fn. 1.

75 *Geblætsod:* for *-blets-,* see Intro. p. 7. *Ealmihtiga:* for *Æl-,* prob-
ably by analogy with the adj. *eal(l)* (SB § 85 Anm. 3).

76 *geeadmed:* for *-met* (as in GO), 3 sg.pres.ind.: the *-d* is probably
restored by analogy with other parts of the vb. (SB § 359 Anm. 2,
Campbell § 482); cp l. 117n below. *þa modigan:* Landferth has *qui
superbos humiliat, qui humiles exaltat. ahæfð:* for *ahefð,* see Intro.
p. 7.

79 *Eft . . . 91 be ðam:* Landferth II (i 10–16), considerably short-
ened, and omitting the account of an accompanying miracle (i 12–14).
ll. 79–88 are very close to the first part of *Epitome* § 6, but there is
nothing in the *Epitome* corresponding to ll. 88–91.

82 *and þære alefednysse:* 'and [the curing] of his infirmity'. The
second of two coordinate genitives often follows the noun modified;
the same is true of genitives in apposition (e.g. I 231) and of co-
ordinate adjectives; cp *Primer* § 100.

85 *gebigdum cneowum:* see I 98 f note.

wearð þa gehæled þurh þone halgan bisceop swa þæt næs
gesyne syððan on his hricge hwær se hofor stode þe hine
gehefegode oð þæt. Þa nyston þa munecas be ðam mæran
halgan and wendon þæt sum oðer halga gehælde þone mann;
90 ac se ceorl sæde þæt Swyðun hine gehælde, for ðan þe he
sylf wiste gewissost be ðam.

Sum wer wæs geuntrumod swiðe yfelum broce, swa þæt
he earfoðlice þa eagan undyde and uneaðe mihte ænig word
gecweðan, ac læg swa geancsumod, orwene his lifes. Ða
95 woldon his freond ealle hine ferian to Niwan Mynstre to
þam halgan Iudoce þæt he him hæle forgeafe; ac him sæde
sum man þæt him selra wære þæt hi to Ealdan Mynstre

95 *freond*] A; *frynd* GO.

---

92 *Sum* . . . 118 *gefremað*: cp Landferth III (i 17–24), *Epitome* end
of § 6 and beginning of § 7: ll. 92–109 represent a considerable
shortening of Landferth i 17–23, which is, however, rather different
from the summary in *Epitome* § 6.

95 *freond*: analogical nom.pl. (see QW § 48, and cp textual notes,
and l. 311n below).

95 *Niwan Mynstre*: the New Minster, Winchester, founded as a
house of clerks by Edward the Elder in 901 (see Philip Grierson,
'Grimbald of St Bertins', EHR lv (1940) 554–7); so called to dis-
tinguish it from the Old Minster, see I 118n. Athelwold replaced the
clerks by monks in 964, see ll. 23–4n above.

96 *þam halgan Iudoce*: St Judoc (in France called St Josse); he was
the son of Juthail (or Judathail), king of Brittany, and lived as a
hermit in Ponthieu, where he died *c*. 668 (see the *Vita* in *Acta
SS.O.S.B.* (1936) ii 565–71). References to the presence of his relics
at the New Minster are fairly frequent from the end of the tenth
century: according to traditions current in the Minster *c*. 1300, they
were brought there at the beginning of the tenth century, when, as
the result of a viking raid on Ponthieu, many of the inhabitants
sought refuge in England. The *adventus S. Iudoci, S. Iudoces tocyme*,
is recorded in Chron. F (*c*. 1100) s.a. 903, and in the *Annales Cices-
trenses* s.a. 902; but the correct date is probably 901 (see Philip
Grierson, *loc.cit.*, 556 f, and TRHS IV xxiii (1941) 78). On the con-
tinent nothing was apparently known of this translation of the relics,
which were believed to be still in France (see T. D. Hardy, *Descriptive
Catalogue* (R.S. 26) i 266–9, and Ordericus Vitalis III c. xiii).

97 *sum man*: in Landferth a man who appeared in a vision to the

þone adligan feredon to Swyðunes byrgene; and hi dydon
swa sona. Hi wacodon ða þa niht wið þa byrgene mid him,
biddende þone ælmihtigan God þæt he ðam adligan menn 100
his hæle forgeafe þurh þone halgan Swyðun. Se untruma
eac wacode oð þæt hit wolde dagian; þa wearð he on
slæpe, and seo wurðfulla byrgen, þæs ðe him eallum þuhte,
eall bifigende wæs, and þam adlian þuhte swylce man his
ænne sco of ðam fet him atuge, and he færlice awoc. 105
He wæs ða gehæled þurh ðone halgan Swyðun, and man
sohte þone sco swyðe geornlice, ac hine ne mihte nan
man gemeten þær æfre; and hi gewendan þa ham mid þam
gehæledan menn. Þær wurdon gehælede æt ðære halgan
byrgene eahta untrume menn ær ðan þe he of ðære byrgene 110
up genumen wære wundorlice þurh God.

Eadgar cyning þa æfter ðysum tacnum wolde þæt se
halga wer wurde up gedon, and spræc hit to Aðelwolde þam
arwurðan bisceope, þæt he hine up adyde mid arwurðnysse.
Þa se bisceop Aðelwold, mid abbodum and munecum, dyde 115
up þone sanct mid sange wurðlice, and bæron into cyrcan

---

98 *dydon swa sona*] A; *swa dydon sona* G. 103 *wurðfulla*] A, -*a*
altered to -*e* by rev.; *wurð*[*ful*]*la* O; *wurðfulle* G. 105 *of ðam fet him*]
A; *of þam fet* G; *of his fet* O. 108 *gemeten*] A, altered to *gemetan* by
rev.; *gemetan* G. 116 *sanct*] AGO, in A *c* inserted above the line.
116 insertion before *cyrcan* erased in G.

---

sick man himself, and who is clearly St Swithin, although not
named.

97 *selra*: nom.sg.neut.def.(wk.), see Intro. p. 10.

103 *wurðfulla*: nom.sg.fem.def.(wk.), see Intro. p. 10, and cp textual
notes.

104 *adlian*: for *adligan*, see Intro. p. 9, fn. 1.

108 *g̈emeten*: inf., see Intro. p. 10, and cp textual notes.

108 *gewendan*: pret.pl., see Intro. p. 10.

116 *bæron*: pl., referring to Athelwold and the abbots and monks.

116 *cyrcan* . . . 117 *huse*: the Old Minster; see I 118n. During the
later Middle Ages it was known as St Swithin's; at the reforma-
tion the dedication was changed to the Holy Trinity. The use of the
dat. *huse* is difficult to explain. Perhaps *on* has dropped out after
cyrcan: the present reading of G is the same as A's, but cp textual
notes; O has *sange* [. . .]*s huse*. On the form *sancte* see I 144n.

Sancte Petres huse, þær he stend mid wurðmynte and
wundra gefremað. Þær wurdon gehælede þurh ðone halgan
wer feower wanhale menn binnan ðrym dagum; and geond
120 fif monþas feawa daga wæron þæt ðær næron gehælede
huru ðry untrume, hwilon fif oððe syx, seofon oððe eahta,
tyn oððe twelf, syxtyne oððe eahtatyne. [B]innon tyn
dagum þær wurdon twa hund manna gehælede, and swa
fela binnan twelf monðum þæt man hi getellan ne mihte.
125 Se lictun læg afylled mid alefedum mannum, swa þæt man
eaðe ne mihte þæt mynster gesecan; and þa ealle wurdon
swa wundorlice gehælede binnan feawa dagum þæt man
þær findan ne mihte fif unhale menn of þam micclan heape.

On þam dagum wæron on Wihtlande þreo wif, þa twa
130 wæron blinde geond nigon geara fec, and þæt þrydde ne
geseah þære sunnan leoht næfre. Hi begeaton þa earfoð-
lice him ænne latteow, ænne dumbne cnapan, and comon
to þam halgan, and ane niht þær wacodon, and wurdon
gehælede, ge ða blindan wif, ge se dumba latteow. Þa sæde
135 se cnapa þam cyrcwerde þæt, and cwæð þæt he næfre ær
naht cweðan ne mihte, and bæd þæt hi sungon þone
gesettan lofsang.

On þære ylcan tide wæs sum wyln gehæft to swinglum for
swyðe lytlan gylte, and læg on hæftnedum þæt heo hetelice

118 þurh ðone halgan] AG, in A written twice, the first time crossed
out. 122 Binnon] GO; binnon A. 123 wurdon] AG; wæron O. 124
þæt man] AO; þæt nan man G, nan altered from man, man inserted in
margin by later hand, insertion after þæt erased. 126 ealle wurdon]
AG; wurdon ealle O. 130 þæt] AG; om. O. 131 næfre] AGO, in A r
altered from another letter. 132 him] AGO, in A inserted by original
scribe.

117 stend: for stent (as in GO), 3 sg.pres.ind.; cp l. 76n above.
118 þær . . . 128 heape: cp Landferth IV (ii 1, 2); for ll. 118–24
cp also Epitome § 7 (last part).
129 On . . . 137 lofsang: from Landferth V (ii 3, 4).
130 fec: for fæc, see Intro. p. 7.
132 him: 'for themselves', reflex.dat. of advantage; cp II 208n.
138 On . . . 148 wurðmynte: from Landferth VI (ii 5).
139 lytlan: dat.sg.m.indef.(strong), see Intro. p. 10.

wære þæs on mergen beswungen; þa wacode heo ealle ða 140
niht and mid wope clypode to ðam halgan Swyðune þæt
he hulpe hire earmre and fram þam reðum swinglum hi
ahredde þurh God. Mid þam þe hit dagode and man
Drihtnes lofsang ongan, þa feollan ða fotcopsas færlice hire
fram; and heo arn to cyrcan to þam arwurðan halgan 145
gebundenum handum swa swa se halga wolde; and se
hlaford com æfter and alysde hire handa and gefreode hi
sona for Swyðunes wurðmynte.

Sum þegn læg alefed lange on paralisyn and ne mihte of
his bedde for manegum gearum. þa cwæð he þæt he wolde 150
to Wynceastre syðian huru on his horsbære and biddan his
hæle. Mid þam þe he þis cwæð to his cnihtum and freondum,
þa wearð he gehæled and gewende swaþeah to þam halgan
sancte, siðigende on fotum fyrmest on þam flocce on ealre
þære fare, and ðancode þam halgan his hæle geornlice. 155

Fif and twentig manna myslice geuntrum[od]e comon
to þam halgan heora hæle biddende: sume wæron blinde,
sume wæron healte, sume eac deafe, and dumbe eac sume;
and hi ealle wurdon anes dæges gehælede þurh þæs halgan
ðingunge and him ham gewendon. 160

Sum þegn wæs on Engla lande on æhtum swyðe welig, se
wearð færlice blind; þa ferde he to Rome: wolde his hæle
biddan æt þam halgum apostolum. He wunode þa on Rome,
and ne wearð gehæled, feower gear fullice, and [g]efran þa

142 *hi*] inserted above the line in A. 150 *þæt he*] AO, in A in-
serted above the line. 151 *his* (first)] A; om. O. 156 *myslice*] A; om.
O. *geuntrumode*] O; *geuntrume* A. 159 *ealle wurdon*] A; *wurdon ealle*
O. 164 *gefran*] O; *befran* A.

143 *Mid þam þe* . . . 144 *ongan:* cp I 95–7n.
149 *Sum* . . . 155 *geornlice:* cp Landferth VII (ii 6).
149 f: on the omission of the inf. of a vb. of motion, see QW
§ 136(a); cp also l. 282 below.
156 *Fif* . . . 160 *gewendon:* from Landferth XIV (ii 17).
156 *geuntrumode:* cp l. 264 below; an adj. *geuntrum* (cp textual
notes) is not otherwise recorded.
161 *Sum* . . . 168 *gesihðe:* from Landferth XVI (ii 18).
164 *feower gear:* Landferth 'five years'.
164 *gefran:* Landferth *audivit; befran* (A) would mean 'enquired'.

165 be Swyðune hwylce wundra he worhte syððan he gewende
þanon. [H]e efste þa swyðe and to his earde gewende and
com to þam halgan were and wearð gehæled þær and ham
gewende mid halre gesihðe.

Sum wer wæs eac blind wel seofon gear fulle, se hæfde
170 ænne latteow þe hine lædde gehwider. [Ð]a sume dæg eode
he swa swa he oft dyde, and se latteow wearð gebolgen and
þone blindan forlet: arn him aweg, and se oðer nyste hu
he ham come, ac clypode to Gode mid innewerdre heortan,
and mid angsumnysse cwæð, 'Eala þu mihtiga Drihten
175 manna and engla, geseoh mine yrmðe: ic geseon ne mæg, and
min lyðra latteow forlet me þus ænne. Gemiltsa me Drihten
þurh ðone mæran Swyðun, and forgif me gesihðe for ðæs
sanctes geearnungum.' Eft he clypode þus, and cwæð to
ðam halgan, 'Eala þu milda bisceop þe manega wundra of
180 cumað þurh þone lifigendan God—leof, ic þe bidde þæt þu
me geþingie to þam mihtigan Hælende: ic gelyfe þæt he
wille gewislice þe tiðian.' He wearð þa gehæled and hæfde
his gesihðe and ham eode blyðe butan latteowe ana, [s]e ðe
lytle ær þanon wæs gelæd þurh ðone oþerne; and his magas
185 ðancodon mycclum ðæs Gode.

Aþelwold þa, se arwurða and se eadiga bisceop, þe on ðam

166 *He*] O; *he* A. 170 *Ða*] *ða* AO. 182 *gewislice*] A; om. O. 183
se] *Se* A. 184 *ðone*] A; om. O.

169 *Sum* . . . 185 *Gode:* from Landferth XVIII (ii 20, 21).

183 *ham eode* . . . *ana:* 'went home alone': see I 193n.

186 *Aþelwold* . . . 218 *gewunon:* cp Landferth X (ii 10–14);
Ælfric's summary is very similar to that in the *Epitome* §§ 9 (ll. 31 ff),
10. There are in addition slight differences between the account given
in Ælfric and the *Epitome*, and that in Landferth: in the latter
Swithin appears to *cuidam venerabili matronæ*, in Ælfric and *Epitome*
to 'a certain good man' (l. 199: *Epitome, cuidam fideli viro*). Further-
more in Ælfric and *Epitome*, the man is told to convey his message
to the monks (l. 199 f: *Epitome, Vade ad monasterium vetus, et dic
fratribus* . . .), although in the event he takes it straight to Athel-
wold: in Landferth this is what the lady is told to do (cp also
ll. 200–1n below). There is, however, nothing in the *Epitome* corre-
sponding to ll. 210 f, 216 f.

dagum wæs on Winceastre bisceop, bead his munecum
eallum þe on ðam mynstre wunodon, þæt hi ealle eodon
endemes to cyrcan and mid sange heredon þæs sanctes
mærða and God mærsodon swa on þam mæran halgan, swa 190
oft swa ænig wanhal mann wurde gehæled. Þa dydon hi
sona swa and sungon þone lofsang oð þæt him laðode
eallum þæt hi swa oft arisan, hwilon þrywa on niht, hwilon
feower syðum, to singenne þone lofsang þonne hi slapan
sceoldon; and forleton [þa] ealle endemes þone sang, for 195
ðam þe se bisceop wæs bysig mid þam cynincge and nyste
butan hi sungon þone lofsang forð on. Hwæt ða se halga
Swyðun sylf com on swefne wundorlice geglencged to
sumum godan menn, and cwæð, 'Gang nu to Ealdan
Mynstre and þam munecum sege þæt Gode swyðe oflicað 200
heora ceorung and slæwð—þæt hi dæghwamlice geseoð
Drihtnes wundra mid him and hi nellað herian þone Hælend
mid sange swa swa se bisceop bebead þam gebroðrum to
donne; and sege gif hi nellað þone sang gelæstan, þonne
geswicað eac sona ða wundra; and gif hi þone lofsang 205
willað æt þam wundrum singan swa oft swa wanhale menn
þær wurðað gerihte, þonne wurðaþ mid him wundra swa
fela þæt nan man ne mæg gemunan on life þæt ænig man
gesawe swylce wundra ahwær.' Þa awæcnode se wer of

191 *wurde*] A; *ðær w*[*urde*] O. 192 *him*] A, altered to *heom* by rev.
195 *þa*] O; om. A. 202 *nellað* . . . 204 *gelæstan*] A; nothing now
legible in O after the first two letters of *ne*[*llað*], until *gelæstan*, but
there is room for about twelve letters only. 209 *awæcnode*] A;
awacode O.

193 *arisan:* pret.pl., see Intro. p. 10.
195 *þa:* cp I 19, II 119.
199 *godan:* dat.sg.masc.indef.(strong), see Intro. p. 10, and cp III
20 f note.
200 *Gode* . . . 201 *dæghwamlice: Epitome, omnipotenti Deo nimium
displicet murmuratio eorum, quoniam quotidie* . . . (Landferth,
displicet omnipotenti Deo, auctori miraculorum, quod quotidie . . .).
202 ff: the scribe of O probably wrote *nellað* (l. 202), and then
resumed after *nellað* (l. 204).

²¹⁰ þam wynsuman slæpe and swyðe besargode þæt he geseon
ne moste, ne nan læncg brucan, þæs beorhtan leohtes þe he
mid Swiðune hæfde gesewen. He aras swaðeah and swiðe
hraðe ferde to Aþelwolde bisceope and him eall þis sæde.
Aþelwold þa asende sona to þam munecum of cyninges
²¹⁵ hyrede and cwæð þæt hi sceoldon þone lofsang singan swa
swa he geset hæfde; and se þe hit forsaw[e], sceolde hit mid
fæstene seofon niht on an swarlice gebetan. Hi hit heoldon
þa syððan symle on gewunon swa swa we gesawon sylfe
foroft, and þone sang we sungon unseldon mid him.
²²⁰ Sum wer wæs betogen þæt he wære on stale: wæs
swaðeah unscyldig; and hine man sona gelæhte and æfter
worulddome dydon him ut þa eagan and his earan forcurfon.
[Þ]a arn him þæt blod into þam heafde þæt he gehyran ne
mihte. þa wæs he seofon monðas wunigende swa blind and
²²⁵ his hlyst næfde, oþ þæt he mid geleafan ferde to þam halgan
Swyðune and gesohte his ban, biddende þone halgan þæt he
his bene gehyrde and him huru geearnode þæt he gehyran

---

210 *þam* . . . 213 *and*] A; nothing now legible in O after the first
letter of *ð*[*am*], until *and*, but there is room for about twelve letters
only.   212 in A insertion erased before *hæfde* and *ða* inserted
before *gesewen* by rev.   216 *forsawe*] AO, in A *-e* on erasure by rev.
219 *him*] A, altered to *heom* by rev.; *heom* O.   223 *þa*] *þa* A.

---

210 ff: the omission in O was perhaps caused by the identical
endings of *slæpe* (l. 210) and *bisceope* (l. 213).
211 *læncg:* for *len*(*c*)*g*, see Intro. p. 7.
218 *gewunon:* dat.sg.masc. *n*-stem, see Intro. p. 10.
218 *swa swa* . . . 219 *him:* Ælfric's addition.
220 *Sum* . . . 235 *hlyst:* from Landferth XXXVIII (ii 54).
221 *æfter worulddome* . . . 222 *forcurfon:* theft was punishable by
death according to the laws of Ælfric's day; but 'the Church favoured
the avoidance of the death-penalty, preferring even the substitution
of mutilation, as this gave the malefactor an opportunity of expiating
his crime in this world and thus saving his soul' (Dorothy Whitelock,
The Beginnings of English Society (1952) 143). Professor Whitelock
suggests that the present passage indicates that the attitude of the
church had had some effect. Cp also Liebermann, *Gesetze*, II 292 f.
On the use of the plural in *dydon* and *forcurfon* see I 159n.

mihte—for þan ðe he ne gelyfde þæt he onliht wurde; and
cwæð þæt he wurde wolice swa getucod. þa wearð Godes
wundor geworht on þam menn þurh Swyðunes þingunge 230
þæt he geseah beorhte ansundum eagum, þeah ðe hi ær
wæron ut aðyde of þam eahhringum, and se oðer æppel
[mid ealle] wæs geemtigod, and se oðer hangode gehal æt his
hleore. Him wæs eac forgifen þæt he wel mihte gehyran, se
ðe ær næfde ne eagan, ne hlyst. Is swaðeah to witenne þæt 235
we ne moton us gebiddan swa to Godes halgum swa swa to
Gode sylfum, for ðan þe he is ana God ofer ealle þincg. Ac
we sceolon biddan soðlice þa halgan þæt hi us þingion to
þam þrymwealdendum Gode, se þe is heora hlaford, þæt he
helpe us.   240
Hwilon wacodon menn, swa swa hit gewunelic is, ofer
an dead lic; and ðær wæs sum dysig mann plegol ungemet-
lice and to þam mannum cwæð, swylce for plegan, þæt he
Swyðun wære: 'Ge magon to soðum witan þæt ic Swyðun
eom se ðe wundra wyrcð and ic wille þæt ge beran eower 245
leoht to me and licgað on cneowum and ic eow forgife þæt

<hr/>

233 *mid ealle*] O; om. A. 234 *hleore*] AO, in A altered from *hreore*
by original scribe. 237 *Ac*] A; *ac* O. 238 *þingion*] A; *geðingian* O.

<hr/>

232 *eahhringum*: for *eag-hringum*, see Campbell § 446.

233 *mid ealle*: Landferth has *Unus autem oculus omnino erat
obrutus*. *geemtigod*: for *geæmtigod*, see Intro. p. 7.

235 *Is . . . 240 us*: Ælfric's addition; on prayers of intercession,
cp CH I 174/9–12, and Thorpe's note (p. 622).

235 *to witenne*: on the apparently passive inf., see QW §§ 131, 136b;
cp l. 254 below. In such expressions a dat.pron. (as at l. 335 below;
cp also I 168 *wanhalum to þicgenne*), is understood; cp also I 80 note.

237 *he is ana God*: transl. 'he alone is God', or 'he is the only God':
see L. Bloomfield, *Language Monographs* VII (1930) 56; cp also
I 193 note. Ælfric's usage differs in some details from Bloomfield's
account.

238 *þingion*: 3 pl.pres.subj., see Intro. p. 11.

239 *þrymwealdendum*: dat.sg.m.def.(wk.), see Intro. p. 11.

241 *Hwilon . . . 262 swiþor*: not in Landferth.

245 *beran*: 2 pl.pres.subj., see Intro. p. 11.

246 *licgað*: apparently 2 pl.pres.ind., although parallel in con-
struction to *beran*; possibly 2 pl.imp., with change of construction.
No reading is available at this point from G or O.

þæt ge gyrnende beoð.' He woffode ða swa lange mid
wordum dyslice oð þæt he feoll geswogen swylce he sawlleas
wære, and hine man bær ham to his bædde sona and he læg
250 swa lange his lifes orwene. His magas ða æt nextan þone
mann feredon to þam halgan Swiþune and he sylf andette
his dyslican word þe he dyrstiglice spræc and bæd him
forgifnysse; and he wearð þa gehæled swa þæt he hal eode
ham mid his magum. Is eac to witenne þæt menn unwis-
255 lice doð þa ðe dwollice plegað æt deadra manna lice and
ælce fulnysse þær forð teoð mid plegan, þonne hi sceoldon
swyðor besargian þone deadan and ondrædan him sylfum
þæs deaðes tocyme and biddan for his sawle butan gewede
georne. Sume menn eac drincað æt deadra manna lice ofer
260 ealle þa niht swiðe unrihtlice and gremiað God mid heora
gegafspræce, þonne nan gebeorscype ne gebyrað æt lice, ac
halige gebedu þær gebyriað swiþor.

Hwilon comon to ðam halgan hundtwelftig manna mis-
lice geuntrumode mid manegum brocum; and þa wurdon
265 ealle wundorlice gehælde binnan þrym wucum and hi wen-
don ham þancigende þam Ælmihtigan and þam arwurðan
Swiþune.

253 *þa*] A; om. O. 255 *plegað*] A, altered to *plegiað* by rev.
261 *gegafspræce*] A; *gafspræcum* O. 263 *ðam*] AO, in A inserted by
rev. 266 *gode* inserted after *ælmihtigan* in A by rev.; om. O.

---

249 *bædde*: for *bedde*, see Intro. p. 7.
254 *Is . . . 262 swiþor*: cp HB I 112–13, where priests are urged to
forbid merrymaking at lyke-wakes and are themselves forbidden to
join in the eating and drinking there. There are also a number of
similarities with the immediately preceding sections (105–10; cp
LS XIII 68–86), forbidding merrymaking in church (cp l. 261n
below).
255 *plegað*: 3 pl.pres.ind. of *plegan*, vocalic (strong) vb. (5), of
which only pres. forms are recorded; the reviser has 'corrected' to the
corresponding form of *plegian*, cons.(wk.) vb. (2).
261 *gegafspræce*: probably -*spræcum* should be read with O, cp
HB I 107 (LS XIII 78), *and mid gegafspræcum Godes hus gefylan*.
263 *Hwilon . . . 267 Swiþune*: cp Landferth XXIII (ii 31) and
Epitome § 9, ll. 11–18; but both Landferth and *Epitome* have 124 sick
men healed in two weeks.

Sumes þegnes cniht feoll færlice of horse þæt him tobærst
se earm and se oðer sceanca, and swiðe wearð gecwysed
þæt hi sona wendon þæt he þærrihte sceolde sweltan him 270
ætforan. He wæs his hlaforde swyþe leof ær þan, and se
hlaford þa besargode swyðe þone cniht and bæd þone
Ælmihtigan mid inwerdre heortan þæt he þam menn
geheolpe þurh ðone mæran Swiþun. He clypode eac to
Swiðune, þus secgende mid geomerunge, 'Eala ðu halga 275
Swiðun, bide þone Hælend þæt he lif forgife þysum lic-
gendum cnihte and ic beo þæs þe geleaffulra þam lifi-
gendan Gode eallum minum dagum gif he deð þis þurh þe.'
Se cniht ða aras hal, gehæled þurh Swiþun, and se hlaford
þæs fægnode and mid geleafan God herede.   280
    Sum eald þegn wæs eac on Wihtlande untrum swa þæt he
læg bæddryda sume nigon gear and of ðam bedde ne mihte
buton hine man bære. Him comon þa on swefne to twegen
scinende halgan and heton hine yrnan ardlice mid him. Þa
cwæð se adliga, '[H]u mæg ic yrnan mid eow þonne ic ne 285
aras of þysum bedde ana nu for nigon gearum butan oþres
mannes fylste?' Þa cwædon þa halgan, '[Þ]u cymst to ðære
stowe gif ðu færst mid us nu, ðær þær ðu underfehst þine
hæle.' He wearð þa swyðe fægen and wolde faran mid him;
ac, þa þa he ne mihte him mid syðian, þa flugon hi geond þa 290
lyft and feredon þone adligan oð þæt hi becomon to sumum

---

268 *his* inserted before *horse* in A by rev.; om. O. 270 *him*] A,
altered to *heom* by rev. 272 *þa*] AO, in A inserted above the line.
274 *geheolpe*] A; *gehulpe* O. 279 *sancte* inserted before *swiþun* in A
by rev.; om. O. *swiþun*] A; *swiðune* O. 282 *bedde*] A, first *e* altered
from *æ* (?). 285 *Hu*] *hu* AO. 287 *Þu*] *þu* AO. 289, 290 *him*] AO, in
A altered to *heom* by rev.

---

268 *Sumes* . . . 280 *herede:* Landferth XXIX (ii 43–5).
    274 *geheolpe:* 3 sg.pret.subj.: the regular form is *gehulpe*, as in O;
cp also *hulpe* l. 142 above.
    276 f *licgendum:* dat.sg.masc.def.(wk.), see Intro. p. 11.
    281 *Sum* . . . 334 *Swiþun:* from Landferth XXXIII (ii 49).
    282 *bæddryda:* for *bedd-*, see Intro. p. 7.
    286 *ana:* 'alone, by myself': see I 193n.

ænlicum felda fægre geblowen; and þær wæs an cyrce of
scinendum golde and of gymstanum standende on þam
felde, and se halga Swiðun on scinendum mæssereafe stod
295 æt ðam weofode, swylce he wolde mæssian.

Swyðun cwæð þa sona to þam seocan menn, 'Ic secge ðe,
broðor, þu ne scealt heononforð nanon menn yfel don, ne
nanne man wyrigan, ne nænne man tælan, ne teonful beon,
ne ðu manslagum ne ðwærlæce ne manfullum reaferum, ne
300 ðeofum þu ne olæce, ne yfeldædum ne geðwærlæce; ac
swiðor gehelp, swa þu selost mæge, wanhafolum mannum
mid þinum agenum spedum—and þu swa þurh Godes
mihte sylf bist gehæled.' Se adliga þa ðohte þæt he yfel
nolde don buton þam anum þe him ær yfel dyde, and þam
305 wolde don wel þe him wel dyde ær. Þa wiste se halga
Swiðun hu his heorte smeade, and cwæð bliðelice him to,
'Broðor, ic þe secge, ne do þu swa þu smeadest þæt ðu
derige ænigum, þeah ðe he derige ðe; ac þinum Drihtne
geefenlæc, se ðe nolde wyrian þa ðe hine [wyrigdon, and

294 *felde*] AO, in A altered to *felda* by rev. *mæssereafe*] AO, in A
mæsse inserted by original scribe. 299 *ðwærlæce*] A, altered to
geðwærlæce by rev.; *gehwær*[. . .] O. 300 *geðwærlæce*] A; [*ge*]-
ðwærlæc O. 303 *Se*] AO, in A *e* altered from *æ*. 307 *Broðor*] A;
broðor O. 309 *wyrigdon* . . . 310 *hine*] [. . . .] *and bæd for ða iude-
iscan þe hine* O, between eight and ten letters are illegible before
and; om. A.

294 *felde*: *-e* for older *-a* may be due to phonetic weakening (see
Intro. p. 10), or transference to the general masc. declension (QW
§ 43); cp textual notes.

297 *nanon*: dat.sg.masc.indef.(strong), see Intro. p. 10.

301 *swa* . . . *mæge*: see II 139n.

304 *buton* . . . *þe*: 'save to him alone who': see I 193n.

309 *wyrigdon* . . . 310 *hine*: the restoration is reasonably certain.
The whole speech is translated fairly closely from the Latin, which
at this point has: *sed potius Dominum imitare Christum, conditorem
rerum, qui cum malediceretur non maledicebat, cum pateretur non
comminabatur, verum pro lædentibus exorabat Patrem* . . . The scribe
of A, having copied the first *ðe hine*, has resumed after the
second.

bæd for ða Iudeiscan þe hine] dydon to cwale, and het his 310
folgeras þæt hi for heora fyond gebædon. Eac cwæð Paulus
se apostol to eallum cristenum mannum, "[G]if ðinum fynd
hingrige, fed hine mid mettum, oððe gif him þyrste, ðu do
him drincan." ' Þa cwæð se bedryda to ðam bisceope eft,
'La leof, sege me hwæt þu sy manna, nu ðu manna heortan 315
miht swa asmeagen.' Þa cwæð se halga Swyðun, '[I]c eom
se þe nu niwan com'—swylce he cwæde swa, '[I]c wæs
geswutelod nu niwan.' Þa cwæð se bædryda to ðam bisceope
eft, '[H]u eart ðu gehaten?'; and se halga him cwæð to,
'Þonne ðu cymst to Winceastre, þu wast minne naman.'   320

Se man wearð þa gebroht to his bedde eft sona and awoc
of slæpe and sæde his wife ealle ða gesihðe þe he gesewen
hæfde. Þa cwæð þæt wif him to þæt hit wære Swyðun se ðe
hine lærde mid þære halgan lare and þone ðe he geseah on
ðære cyrcan swa fægerne. Heo cwæð ða to þam were, 325
'[H]it wære nu full good þæt ðe man bære to cyrcan and þu
bæde þone halgan þæt he ðe gehælde þurh his halgan
geearnunge.' Hine man bær ða sona of ðam bedde to cyrcan
binnan Wihtlande and he wearð gehæled sona þurh þone
ælmihtigan God for Swyðunes geearnungum and eode him 330
ða ham hal on his fotum, se ðe ær wæs geboren on bære to

311 *fyond*] A, altered to *fyondum* by rev.; *fynd* O. 312 *Gif*]
gif AO. 316, 317 *Ic*] *ic* A. 317 *cwæde swa*] A; *swa cwæde* GO. 319
Hu] *hu* AGO. 324 *þære*] AGO, in A æ altered from *a*, and *re* on erasure
(by rev.?). 326 *Hit*] *hit* AG. *ðe man bære*] A; *man þe bære* G; [. . .] *þe*
bære O. 328 *geearnunge*] AGO, in A altered to *geearnunga* by rev.
330 *man* inserted above the line before *swiðhunes* in G; om. A. 331
hal] AG; om. O.

311 *fyond*: acc.pl., probably a mixture of the regular form *fynd*
(cp textual notes, and I 22), and the analogical *feond* (cp l. 95n above).
Alternatively it may be a Kentish spelling for the latter (cp Camp-
bell § 298 and Intro. p. 7, fn. 4).
312 *Gif* . . . 314 *drincan*: Romans 12²⁰.
316 *asmeagen*: inf., see Intro. p. 10.
318 *bædryda*: for *bed-*, see Intro. p. 7.
328 *geearnunge*: acc.pl., see Intro. p. 10, and cp textual notes.

cyrcan. He ferde eac siððan to Ceastre forraðe and cydde
Aðelwolde þam arwurþan bisceope hu he wearð gehæled
þurh þone halgan Swiþun and Landferð se ofersæwisca hit
335 gesette on Læden. Nu is [us] to witenne þæt we ne sceolan
cepan ealles to swyðe be swefnum, for ðan þe hi ealle ne
beoð of Gode. Sume swefna syndon soðlice of Gode, swa swa
we on bocum rædað, and sume beoð of deofle to sumum
swicdome, hu he ða sawle forpære; ac his gedwimor ne
340 mæg derian þam godum, gif hi hi bletsiaþ and hi gebidda[ð]
to Gode. Þa swefna beoð wynsum[e] þe gewurðaþ of Gode,
and þa beoð egefulle ðe of þam deofle cumað; and God sylf
forbead þæt we swefnum ne folgion, þe læs ðe se deofol us
bedydrian mæge.

345 Sum man on Winceastre wearð yrre his ðeowan men for
sumere gymeleaste and gesette hine on fetera. He sæt ða
swa lange on þam laðum bendum, oð þæt he bestæl ut mid

332 *ceastre*] AGO, in AG altered to *winceastre*, in A by rev., in G
by later hand. 335 *us*] GO; om. A. 337 *syndon*] AG; *beoð* O. *soðlice
of gode*] AG; *of gode soðlice* O. 339 *forpære*] AO; *forræde* G. 340 *gebid-
dað*] AGO, in A *ð* by rev. on erasure. 341 *wynsume*] AGO, in A *e*
by rev. on erasure. 343 f *us bedydrian*] AGO, in A by original scribe
on erasure.

332 *Ceastre:* i.e. Winchester; on the use of the simple form in place
of the more specific cpd., see Plummer ii 32.

332 *forraðe:* for *forhraðe*, see Intro. p. 9.

334 *Landferð* . . . 335 *Læden:* Ælfric's addition, which may have
been suggested by Landferth's reference at this point to the fact that
this miracle was related to him by Athelwold himself; on Landferth
see Intro. p. 20.

335 *Læden:* probably for *Leden*, cp Bülbring § 178, and Intro. p. 7.

335 *Nu* . . . 344 *mæge:* Ælfric's addition.

335 *us:* the reading of GO is rhythmically preferable; cp III 235n.
sceolan: pres.pl., see Intro. p. 10.

343 *forbead* . . . *folgion:* 'forbade us to be guided by dreams': the
construction with negative in the dependent clause is normal in OE.
The reference is possibly to Jeremiah 29[8]. *folgion:* pres.subj.pl., see
Intro. p. 11.

345 *Sum* . . . 350 *halgan:* Landferth XXXV (ii 51).

his stafe hoppende and gesohte ðone sanct Swyðun mid
geomerunge. Se scyttel ða asceat sona of þære fetere and se
ðeowa aras ahred þurh ðone halgan.   350
   Sum mann wæs gebunden onbutan þæt heafod for his
hefigum gylte, se com to þam halgan and his swara heafod-
bend sona tobærst swa he hine gebæd.
   Ne mage we awritan, ne mid wordum asecgan, ealle þa
wundra þe se halga wer Swiðun þurh God gefremode on ðæs 355
folces gesihþe, ge on [ge]hæftum mannum, ge on unhalum
mannum, mannum to swutelunge þæt hi sylfe magon Godes
rice geearnian mid godum weorcum swa swa Swiþun dyde,
þe nu scinð þurh wundra. Seo ealde cyrce wæs eall behangen
mid criccum and mid creopera scamelum fram ende oð 360
oþerne on ægðrum wage, þe ðær wurdon gehælede; and
man ne mihte swaðeah macian hi healfe up. Þyllice tacna
cyþað þæt Crist is Ælmihtig God, þe his halgan geswutelode
þurh swylce weldæda, þeah ðe ða Iudeiscan, þurh deofol

348 hoppende] AO; hoppegende G. 356 gehæftum] AGO, in A ge in-
serted by rev. mannum] A; om. G. 360 scamelum] A, altered to
sceamelum by rev.; sceamelum GO.

348 stafe: for stæfe (as in GO), see SB § 240 Anm. 2. hoppende: the
form in G is probably for hoppigende, pres.pt. of a cons.(wk.)vb. (2),
recorded once elsewhere (CH I 202/18); that in AO from a cons.
(wk.)vb. (1), not otherwise recorded.
   351 Sum . . . 353 gebæd: perhaps from Landferth XXIV (ii 32),
if so, much abbreviated. The man in Landferth's chapter wore nine
fetters, one round his waist and another round his arm: where the
others were is not stated.
   354 Ne mage . . . 368 gelyfan: not directly from Landferth or
Epitome.
   356 gehæftum: hæft (cp textual notes) is not otherwise recorded as
adj.
   362 tacna: nom.pl., see Intro. p. 10.
   364 ff: Ælfric frequently refers to the coming of Antichrist and the
Last Judgement, e.g. CH I 2 ff, 608 ff, II 536 ff, LS XXXV 347 ff;
cp also Dorothy Bethurum, The Homilies of Wulfstan (1957) 278 ff.
He refers again at LS XXV 527 to the common medieval belief that
the remnant of the Jews would be converted on the last day; on the
Jews see also II 223n.

365 beswicene, nellon gelyfan on þone lyfigendan Crist, ær ðan
þe Antecrist ofslagen bið þurh God; þonne bugað þa
earmingas on ende þysre worulde, ðe þær to lafe beoð, mid
geleafan to Criste, and ða ærran losiað þe ær noldon gelyfan.
We habbað nu gesæd be Swiðune þus sceortlice, and we
370 secgað to soðan þæt se tima wæs gesælig and wynsum on
Angelcynne, þa ða Eadgar cynincg þone cristendom
gefyrðrode and fela munuclifa arærde, and his cynerice wæs
wunigende on sibbe, swa þæt man ne gehyrde gif ænig
scyphere wære, buton agenre leode þe ðis land heoldon,
375 and ealle ða cyningas þe on þysum iglande wæron, Cumera
and Scotta, comon to Eadgare—hwilon anes dæges eahta
cyningas—and hi ealle gebugon to Eadgares wissunge.

365 *crist*] A; *god* G. 366 *ofslagen*] A; *acweald* GO. 371 *angelcynne*]
AG, in G *cynne* inserted above the line by original scribe. 374 *heol-
don*] A; *geheoldon* O. 375 *þe*] A; om. O. 377 *cyningas*] AO, in A *s*
altered from another letter.

365 *nellon:* pres.subj.pl., see Intro. p. 11.

369 *We . . .* 386 *hi:* not from Landferth or *Epitome*. These lines
should be compared with Ælfric's other references to the glorious
reign of Edgar in the epilogue to *Judges* (ed. Crawford, *Heptateuch*,
416 f/82–7); in LS XIII 147–51; and in the opening lines of the
present homily (cp also the Ely charter which may be by Ælfric,
on which see Angus McIntosh, *Wulfstan's Prose* (1949) 113 and
note 8). The poems in the Chronicle s.a. 959 DE and, in part, F, and
975 DE, should also be compared: the first of these is by Wulfstan
(on other references to Edgar by Wulfstan see Dorothy Bethurum,
op.cit., 82–3).

371 *Eadgar . . .* 372 *arærde:* Edgar identified himself completely
with the work of the English monastic reformers: more than twenty
monasteries were founded or reformed during his reign. On the term
munuclif see I 91–2n.

373 *swa þæt . . .* 374 *heoldon:* in striking contrast to the situation
at the time when Ælfric was writing: Ælfric refers to the viking
invasions in his own time in CH I 578 f; II 1, 370; and LS XIII
152–5, where he attributes them to the persecution of the mon-
asteries after Edgar's death.

375 *ealle . . .* 377 *wissunge:* cp Chron. s.a. 972 DEF. This event is
also referred to in the epilogue to *Judges*, the Ely charter, and the
Chron. poems s.a. 959, 975 (see ll. 369–86n above; for later references
see Plummer ii 162); on its significance see Stenton 364 f.

ST SWITHIN, BISHOP

Þærtoeacan wæron swilce wundra gefremode þurh þone
halgan Swyðun, swa swa we sædon ær, and swa lange swa
we leofodon, þær wurdon gelome wundra. On ðam timan 380
wæron eac wurðfulle bisceopas—Dunstan se anræda æt
ðam ercestole, and Aþelwold se arwurða, and oðre ge-
hwylce; ac Dunstan and Aþelwold wæron Drihtne gecorene,
and hi swyðost manodon menn to Godes willan, and ælc god
aræðdon Gode to [ge]cwemednysse: þæt geswuteliað þa 385
wundra þe God wyrcð þurh hi. Sy wuldor and lof þam
welwillendan Scyppende, þe his halgan mærsað mihtiglice
mid wundrum, se ðe a[na] rixað on ecnysse. Amen.

385 *gecwemednysse*] *ge*[*cwemednysse*] O; *cwemednysse* A. 386 *Sy* . . .
388 *AMEN*] the doxology follows at this point in A and O, but in A
is marked by the rev. to be transposed to the end of the next item in
the MS. 388 *ana*] O; *a* A.

---

381 *Dunstan* . . . 382 *Aþelwold:* on Dunstan see Intro. p. 19; on
Athelwold see l. 14n above; cp also Ælfric's preface to his *Grammar:
Dunstan arcebisceop and Aðelwold bisceop eft þa lare on munuclifum
aræðdon* (ed. Zupitza 3/15 f).
   385 *gecwemednysse:* the form without the prefix (cp textual notes)
is not otherwise recorded.
   388 *ana:* the same doxology at the end of Assmann IV; the same
formula with *æfre* (but not *a*) in place of *ana* occurs several times
(e.g. LS IX, XI, XXVII, Assmann VIII).

SELECT BIBLIOGRAPHY

I. FACSIMILE

*1861 John Earle, *Gloucester Fragments* (see above p. 5, fn. 7).

II. EDITIONS

(i) LIVES OF SAINTS

*†1881–1900 W. W. Skeat, *Ælfric's Lives of Saints* (E.E.T.S., O.S. 76, 82, 94, 114) (see above pp. 1, fn. 2, 12, fn. 1).

The homilies on St Oswald and St Edmund are printed in various readers, of which the most important are:

1834 Benjamin Thorpe, *Analecta Anglo-Saxonica* (*St Edmund*, from MS B) 2nd ed. 1846.

1876 Henry Sweet, *An Anglo-Saxon Reader* (*St Oswald*, from MS A) 9th–14th edd. (revised by C. T. Onions) 1922–59.

1882 Henry Sweet, *An Anglo-Saxon Primer* (*St Edmund*) 9th ed. (revised by Norman Davis) 1953.

(ii) OTHER WORKS BY ÆLFRIC

*1844–6 B. Thorpe, *The Homilies of the Anglo-Saxon Church*, 2 vols.

1880 J. Zupitza, *Ælfrics Grammatik und Glossar* (Berlin).

†1883–4 G. E. MacLean, 'Ælfric's Version of Alcuini Interrogationes Sigeuulfi in Genesin', *Anglia* vi 425–73; vii 1–59.

†1885 B. Assmann, *Abt Ælfric's Angelsächsische Bearbeitung des Buches Esther* (Halle, Diss.); cp *Anglia* ix (1886), 25–38.

†1888 B. Assmann, 'Abt Ælfrics as. Homilie über das Buch Judith', *Anglia* x 76–104.

†1889 B. Assmann, *Angelsächsische Homilien und Heiligenleben* (Bibl. der as. Prosa iii) (nos. I–IX are by Ælfric).

†1891 A. Tessmann, *Aelfrics Altenglische Bearbeitung der Interrogationes Sigewulfi Presbyteri in Genesin des Alcuin* (Berlin, Diss.).

*†1914 B. Fehr, *Die Hirtenbriefe Ælfrics* (Bibl. der as. Prosa ix).

*†1921 S. J. Crawford, *Exameron Anglice* (Bibl. der as. Prosa x).

*†1922 S. J. Crawford, *The Old English Version of the Heptateuch, etc* (E.E.T.S., O.S. 160).

†1938 G. N. Garmonsway, *Ælfric's Colloquy*.

†1942 H. Henel, *De Temporibus Anni*, (E.E.T.S., O.S. 213).

III. TRANSLATIONS

Works listed here marked *.

BIBLIOGRAPHY

IV. STUDIES AND NOTES

General histories of Old English literature are not included in the list.

Works cited above marked †.

(i) GENERAL

References to studies earlier than Dietrich's (which are of little value) can be found in White (1899) and Dubois (1943).

1855-6 E. F. Dietrich, 'Abt Ælfric', *Zeitschrift für die historische Theologie* xxv 487–594; xxvi 163–256.

1898 C. L. White, *Ælfric, a new study of his life and writings* (Yale Studies in English 2).

1912 S. H. Gem, *An Anglo-Saxon Abbot, Ælfric of Eynsham* (Edinburgh).

1927 K. Jost, 'Unechte Ælfrictexte', *Anglia* li 81–103, 177–219.

1931-3 K. Sisam, 'MSS Bodley 340, 342: Ælfric's Catholic Homilies', RES vii 7 ff; viii 51 ff; ix 1 ff. Reprinted in *Studies in the History of Old English Literature* (1953) 148–98, with an additional note on 'The Order of Ælfric's Books' 298–301.

1940 A. A. Prins, 'Some Remarks on Ælfric's Lives of Saints and his Translations from the Old Testament', *Neophilologus* xxv 112 ff.

1943 D. Whitelock, 'Two Notes on Ælfric and Wulfstan', MLR xxxviii 122–6.

1943 M.-M. Dubois, *Ælfric, Sermonnaire, Docteur et Grammarien* (Paris).

1952 J. Raith, 'Ælfric's Share in the Old English Pentateuch', RES NS iii 305 ff.

1959 P. A. M. Clemoes, 'The Chronology of Ælfric's works', *The Anglo-Saxons, Studies . . . presented to Bruce Dickins*, ed. Peter Clemoes, 212–47.

(ii) SOURCES

Only those discussions which are of immediate relevance to the homilies edited in this volume are included. For editions of the sources of the homilies edited here, see above pp. 18, fnn. 2, 4; 19, fn. 3.

1892 J. H. Ott, *Ueber die Quellen der Heiligenleben in Ælfrics Lives of Saints I* (Halle, Diss.).

1909 G. H. Gerould, 'Ælfric's Legend of St Swithin', *Anglia* xxxii 346–57.

1931 Grant Loomis, 'Further Sources of Ælfric's Saints Lives', HSN xiii 1–8.

1932 Grant Loomis, 'The Growth of the Saint Edmund Legend', HSN xiv 83–113.

1933 Grant Loomis, 'Saint Edmund and the Lodbrok (Lothbroc) Legend', HSN xv 1-23.

(iii) STYLE

Discussions of Ælfric's alliterative style prior to the appearance of Skeat's edition of the *Lives of Saints* are mentioned in the first item in the list below.

1883 E. Holthaus, Review of Skeat's edition of the *Lives of Saints* Part I, *Anglia* vi, Anzeiger 104-17.

1888 A. Reum, 'De Temporibus, Ein echtes Werk des Abtes Ælfric', *Anglia* x 457-98.

1896-7 A. Brandeis, 'Die Alliteration in Ælfrics metrischen Homilien', *Jahres-Bericht der K.K. Staats-Realschule im VII Bezirke in Wien* (Wien) 3-32.

1925 G. H. Gerould, 'Abbot Ælfric's rhythmic prose', MP xxii 353-66.

1932 D. Bethurum, 'The form of Ælfric's Lives of the Saints' SP xxix 515-33.

1949 Angus McIntosh, 'Wulfstan's Prose', *Proceedings of the British Academy* xxxv 109-142.

1962 O. Funke, 'Studien zur alliterierenden und rhythmisierenden prosa in der älteren altenglischen homiletik', *Anglia* lxxx 9-36.

(iv) LANGUAGE

1886 Th. Wohlfahrt, *Die Syntax des Verbums in Ælfric's Uebersetzung des Heptateuch und des Buches Hiob* (München, Diss.).

1887 A. S. Cook, 'List of the Strong Verbs in Part II of Ælfric's Saints', MLN ii 117 f.

1887 B. Schrader, *Studien zur Ælfricschen Syntax* (Jena).

1888 B. J. Wells, 'Strong Verbs in Ælfric's Judith', MLN iii 13-15.

1888 B. J. Wells, 'Strong Verbs in Ælfric's Saints', MLN iii 178-85, 256-62.

1888-9 F. Fischer, 'The stressed vowels in Ælfric's Homilies', PMLA iv 194-213.

1889 P. Th. Kühn, *Die Syntax des Verbums in Ælfrics 'Heiligenleben'* (Leipzig, Diss.).

1890 M. Braunschweiger, *Flexion des Verbums in Älfrics Grammatik* (Marburg, Diss.).

1892 C. Brühl, *Die Flexion des Verbums in Ælfrics Heptateuch und Buch Hiob* (Marburg, Diss.).

1893 G. Schwerdtfeger, *Das schwache Verbum in Ælfrics Homilien* (Marburg, Diss.).

1904 H. Brüll, *Die ae. Latein-Grammatik des Ælfric* (Berlin).

BIBLIOGRAPHY

1905 J. Wilkes, 'Lautlehre zu Ælfrics Heptateuch und Buch Hiob', *Bonner Beiträge* xxi.
1908 O. Schüller, *Lautlehre von Aelfric's 'Lives of Saints'* (Bonn, Diss.).
1932 N. O. Halvorson, 'Doctrinal Terms in Ælfric's Homilies', *University of Iowa Humanistic Studies* V (1932–8) no. 1.
1933 T. R. Göhler, *Lautlehre der ae. Hexameron Homilie des Abtes Ælfrik* (München).
1934-5 P. Meissner, 'Studien zum Wortschatz Ælfrics', *Archiv* clxv 11–19; clxvi 30–9, 205–15.
1953 C. R. Barrett, *Studies in the Word-Order of Ælfric's Catholic Homilies and Lives of the Saints* (Cambridge).

ADDITIONAL BIBLIOGRAPHY

This list is restricted to publications of immediate relevance to the homilies edited above. For information regarding other published work on Ælfric the bibliographies in the last item on the list may be consulted.

1907 Lord Francis Hervey, *Corolla Sancti Eadmundi, the Garland of Saint Edmund* (London). [An extensive collection of material relating to St Edmund, including Ælfric's homily and Abbo's life, both with translation.]
1964 T. Wolpers, *Die englische Heiligenlegende des Mittelalters: eine Formgeschichte des Legendenerzählens von der spätantiken lateinischen Tradition bis zur Mitte des 16. Jahrhunderts* (Tübingen).
1965 J. E. Cross, 'Oswald and Byrhtnoth', *English Studies* xlvi 93-109.
1966 P. A. M. Clemoes, 'Ælfric', *Continuations and Beginnings*, ed. E. G. Stanley, 176-209.
1967-8 J. C. Pope, *Homilies of Ælfric: a Supplementary Collection* (E.E.T.S. 259, 260).
1968 C. Clark, 'Ælfric and Abbo', *English Studies* xlix 30-36.
1971 R. Torkar, 'Zu den Vorlagen der ae. Handschrift Cotton Julius E vii', *Neuphilologische Mitteilungen* lxxii 711-715.
1972 J. Hurt, *Ælfric* (Twayne's English Authors Series 131) (New York).
1972 M. Winterbottom, *Three Lives of English Saints* (Toronto). [Contains the lives of Æthelwold by Ælfric and Wulfstan and the life of St Edmund by Abbo.]
1974 C. L. White, *Ælfric: a new study of his life and writings* reprinted with a supplementary classified bibliography prepared by M. R. Godden (Hamden, Connecticut).

GLOSSARY

In the glossary words will be found under the forms in which they
occur in the text, with the following exceptions: words spelt with
i or *y* are entered under the most frequently occurring form and there
is no cross-reference under the alternative spelling; variation be-
tween *þ* and *ð* is disregarded: *þ* is always used initially and *ð* else-
where; nouns are entered under the nom.sg., pronouns of the 1st and
2nd persons sg. and pl. under the nom., adjectives and the remaining
pronouns under the nom.sg.m., and verbs under the inf. (except for
a few defective verbs which are entered under the 1 sg.pres. or pret.,
e.g. *dearr, mōt, ēode, wæs, næs,* etc).

Reference to the text is by homily and line number; italicized line
numbers refer to the textual variants. An n after a line number
indicates that there is a comment on the word in the note on that
line. An * after a line number indicates a restored or emended form.

The order of letters is alphabetical; *æ* is treated as a separate letter
after *a*; *þ,ð* after *t*. The prefix *ge-* is ignored in the arrangement of the
glossary. For the abbreviations used in this series see *Deor,* p. 32, or
Waldere, p. 49.

Reference is made to the *New English Dictionary* by printing the
NED word (under which the OE word is discussed) as the first meaning
in capitals; if the word is not the true phonological descendant of the
OE form in the glossary it is italicized. Unless it provides the mean-
ing required by the context it is followed by a semi-colon and the
meaning required in ordinary lower-case type. If is it radically
different in meaning or if it is obsolete or archaic it is enclosed in
square brackets. Unless otherwise stated, the NED reference is to
the same part of speech as the word in the glossary.

A

ā, *adv.* [O]; for ever I 36, etc.

abbod, *m.a-stem, ABBOT* II 12,
III 115.

abēodan, *v.(2),* [ABEDE]; de-
clare, deliver II 42, III 30, 64.

abīdan, *v.(1),* ABIDE; remain I
207; *w.gen.* await II *154.*

abūgan, *v.(2),* [ABOW]; submit,
yield II 17, 40, 78; turn aside
II 69.

abūtan, *adv.* ABOUT; round II
169.

abyrian, *w.v.(1b), w.gen.* taste
II 132.

ac, *conj.* [AC]; but I 12, 66, etc.

acwellan, *w.v.(1c),* [AQUELL];
kill III 366.

ādlig, *adj.* [ADLE *sb.* + -Y¹]; sick
I 167, etc; *as sb.* I 31, 217, etc.

adōn, *anom.v.* [A- + DO]; *a-
dydon up,* exhumed III 114.

adræfan, *w.v.(1b),* [ADREFE];
expel III 24.

adrēogan, *v.(2),* [ADREE]; *a-
dreah his lif,* spent his life I
202.

adwǣscan, *w.v.(1b),* extinguish
I 11.

afaran, v.(6), [AFARE]; depart II 113.

aflīgan, w.v.(1b), [AFLEY]; expel I 164.

afȳlan, w.v.(1b), [AFILE]; defile II 74.

afyllan, w.v.(1b), [AFILL]; fill III 125.

afyllan, w.v.(1b), [AFELLE]; kill I 17.

afyrht, adj.(p.pt.), [AFFRIGHT]; terrified I 156, 191.

āgen, adj. OWN I 53, II 68, III 302, 374.

agēotan, v.(2), [AGETEN]; pour away I 162.

ahebban, v.(6), [AHEAVE]; exalt II 20, III 76.

ahōn, v.(7), [AHANG]; hang I 186, 192.

a(h)rǣran, w.v.(1b), [AREAR]; raise up II 207; erect I 14, 71n, etc; establish I 114, III 385.

ahreddan, w.v.(1a), [AREDDE]; save I 17, 19, III 143; release III 350.

āhwǣr, adv. [OWHERE]; anywhere II 121, III 209.

ahyldan, w.v.(1b), [A- + HIELD]; bend, turn II 18.

alecgan; alēdon, pret.pl. I 22; w.v.(1c), ALLAY¹; lay low.

alēfed, adj. disabled III 125, 149.

alēfednys(s), f.jō-stem, disability III 82.

alēogan, v.(2), w.acc. of thing promised and dat. of person to whom promise is made, [A- + LIE²]; fail to perform I 222.

alȳsan, w.v.(1b), [ALESE]; release III 147; alys ut, release II 181.

ān, I 199, etc; ǣnne, acc.sg.m. I 187, etc; āna III 183, etc; āne II 64n, nom.sg.m.wk.; adj. ONE II 106, etc; A, a certain

I 14, 75n, etc; alone I 193n, etc; w.numeral, some II 202; pron. one I 76; on an, [ANON]; continuously III 217.

geancsumian, w.v.(2), afflict III 94.

and, conj. AND I 4, 5, etc.

andbidian, w.v.(2), w.gen. await II 154.

andettan, w.v.(1b), confess III 251.

an(d)sund, adj. [AND- + SOUND]; unimpaired I 193, etc; uncorrupted II 154, 217, etc; cured I 180*.

andswarian, andswyrde, pret. sg. II 126, iandswæred, p.pt. II 83; w.v.(2), ANSWER II 127.

andwerd, adj. present II 154.

andwyrdan, w.v.(1b), [AND-WURDE]; answer II 51, 83, etc.

angsumnys(s), f.jō-stem, distress III 174.

geānlǣcan, w.v.(1b), unite I 90, II 28.

ānmōdlīce, adv. [ANMOD + LY²]; resolutely III 43.

ānrǣde, adj. [ANRED]; steadfast II 17, 103, III 381.

ansund, see an(d)sund.

apostol, m.a-stem, APOSTLE III 163, 312.

arǣran, see a(h)rǣran.

ardlīce, adv. swiftly, immediately II 42, 46, etc.

ārian, w.v.(2), w.dat. [ARE¹]; have mercy on II 191.

arīsan, v.(1), ARISE I 174, III 82, 193n, etc.

ārlēas, adj. impious, wicked II 101n; as sb. II 83, 91.

ārwurð, adj. [ARE sb.¹ + WORTH]; venerable I 44, II 166, III 20, etc.

ārwurðian, w.v.(2), [ARE sb.¹ + WORTH]; honour I 122.

ārwurŏllĭce, *adv.* [ARE *sb.*[1] + WORTHLY]; with honour I 50, 143, 159.

ārwurŏnys(s), *f.jō-stem*, [ARE *sb.*[1] + WORTHNESS]; honour I 157, III 114.

ascēotan, *v.(2)*, [A- + SHOOT]; shoot out III 349.

asecgan, *w.v.(3)*, [A- + SAY[1]]; recount III 354.

asendan, *w.v.(1b)*, [ASEND]; send II 122; send (a message) III 214.

aslēan, *v.(6)*, [ASLAY]; of aslean, strike off I 135, 145.

asmēagan, *w.v.(2)*, understand III 316n; conceive II 213.

asmiŏian, *w.v.(2)*, [A- + SMITH]; make I 144.

aspringan, *v.(3)*, [ASPRING]; spread I 197.

astreccan, *w.v.(1c)*, [ASTRETCH]; extend I 153.

astyrian, *w.v.(1a)*, [ASTIR]; reflex. move II 174.

atēon, *v.(2)*, [ATEE]; lift III 37, etc; remove III 105.

aŏwēan, *v.(6)*, wash I 162.

aŏȳn, *w.v.(1b)*, thrust out III 232.

awacian, *w.v.(2)*, AWAKE III 209.

awæcnan, *v.(6)*, AWAKE(N) I 180, III 105, 321.

awæcnian, *w.v.(2)*, AWAKE(N) III 209.

awǣgan, *w.v.(1b)*, repudiate I 221.

awēdan, *w.v.(1b)*, [AWEDE]; go mad II 196.

aweg, *adv.* AWAY I 191, II 81, III 172.

awendan, *w.v.(1b)*, [AWEND]; turn I 51, 98, 208; translate II 10.

awēstan, *w.v.(1b)*, [AWEST]; lay waste II 30.

awrītan, *v.(1)*, [AWRITE]; set down in writing III 8, 354.

awurpan, *v.(3)*, [AWARP]; cast out I 45; cast aside II 88.

awyrigan, *w.v.(1b)*, [AWORRY]; damn II 223.

ģeāxian, *w.v.(2)*, [ASK]; discover I 148.

Æ

æfre, *adv.* EVER II 70, etc; all the time I 90, 98, etc.

æfter, *prep.w.dat.* AFTER I 10, 95, 136, etc; *adv.* after her III 147; **æfter ŏan ŏe**, *conj.* after I 1.

æftergenga, *m.n-stem*, successor I 8n.

ægŏer, *adj.* EITHER, each (of two) III 361.

ægŏyrl, *n.a-stem*, [EYE-THURL]; window II 170n.

æht, *f.i-stem*, [AUGHT[1]]; possession(s) III 161.

ælc, *pron.* EACH I 81, etc; *adj.* every II 159, etc; any I 142.

ælmesgeorn, *adj.* [ALMS + YERN]; diligent in almsgiving I 69.

ælmihtig, ealmihtig, III 75n; *adj.* ALMIGHTY II 69, 207, 221, etc; *as sb.* I 16, 236, etc.

ælmysse, *f.n-stem*, ALMS; almsgiving I 76, 78.

ænig, *adj.* ANY I 211, II 185, etc; *pron.* II 128, III 308.

ænlĭc, *adj.* [ONLY]; magnificent I 91, III 292.

ænne, see ān.

æppel, *m.a-stem*, APPLE; eyeball III 232.

ǣr, *adv.* [ERE]; before, previously I 92,*126, etc; *adj.* early I 20*n; *prep.w.dat.* *(instr.)*, before III 271; **ǣr** þan (þam) þe, *conj.* before I 14 f, II 3*n, etc; **æ̂rra**, *comp. adj.* [ERER]; *as sb.* those who lived in former times III 368; **æ̂rest**, *sup.adv.* [ERST]; first II 8o.

ærcebisceop, *m.a-stem*, ARCHBISHOP II 3.

æ̂rende, *n.ja-stem*, ERRAND; message II 39, 42, III 30.

æ̂rendfæst, *adj.* bound on an errand I 183.

æ̂rendraca, *m.n-stem*, messenger II 41, 72, 81.

æ̂rist, *m.or n.i-stem*, [ARIST]; resurrection II 155.

æsc, *m.a-stem*, [ASH[1]]; (viking) warship II 29n.

æt, *prep.w.dat.* AT I 126, 186, etc; *biddan æt*, ask of III 163.

æteowian, *w.v.(2)*, [ATEW]; show II 194; appear III 21.

ætforan, *prep.w.dat.* [ATFORE]; *postponed*, in front of III 271.

ætgædere, *adv.* together I 73, II 202.

ætstandan, *v.(6)*, [ATSTAND]; remain standing I 193.

æðele, *adj.* [ATHEL]; virtuous I 2, 82, II 15, etc.

æðelincg, *m.a-stem*, [ATHELING]; prince II 34.

B

bān, *n.a-stem*, BONE I 117, 148, 151, etc.

gebædhūs, *n.a-stem*, [BEAD *sb.* + HOUSE[1]]; chapel II 145n.

bær, *f.ō-stem*, BIER; litter III 331.

be, *prep.w.dat.* BY I 103, 144, etc; about II 5, 199, 204, etc.

bearn, *n.a-stem*, [BAIRN]; child II 66.

bēatan, *v.(7)*, BEAT[1] II 92.

bebēodan, *v.(2)*, *w.dat. of person*, [BIBEDE]; command II 84, III 64, etc.

bebod, *n.a-stem*, [BIBOD]; command I 201n, III 72.

bebyrigan, *w.v.(1b)*, [BEBURY]; inter I 116, II 112, etc.

beclyppan, *w.v.(1a)*, [BECLIP[1]]; clasp II 131.

becuman, *v.(4)*, [BECOME]; come I 1, 47, 106, etc.

gebed, *n.a-stem*, [BEAD]; prayer I 20, 93, 97, etc.

bedǣlan, *w.v.(1b)*, [BEDEAL]; deprive II 214.

bedd, *n.ja-stem*, BED I 28, II 65n, III 249n, etc.

bed(d)ryda, *adj.* [BEDRID]; *BEDRIDDEN* III 282n; *as sb.* III 314, 318n.

bedydrian, *w.v.(2)*, [BEDIDDER]; delude III 344.

befri(g)nan, *v.(1),orig.(3)*, [BE-+FRAYNE]; enquire III 164n.

bēgen, *adj.* [BO]; both I 129.

beginnan, *v.(3)*, BEGIN[1] I 92n, 178.

begitan, *v.(5)*, [BEGET]; obtain III 131.

behātan, *v.(7)*, [BEHIGHT]; promise I 104, 221.

behēafdian, *w.v.(2)*, BEHEAD II 103.

behealdan, *v.(7)*, BEHOLD, watch I 154.

behōn, *v.(7)*, [BEHANG]; hang round III 359.

behrēowsian, *w.v.(2)*, [BIREUSY]; repent II 187.

behy̆dan, *w.v.(1b)*, [BEHIDE]; conceal II 108, 110, 118.

belǣfan; bileafe, *pres. 1 sg.* II 64; *w.v.(1b)*, [BELEAVE]; be left.

belīfan, *v.(1)*, [BELIVE]; remain behind II 31, 64.

bēn, *f.i-stem,* [BENE]; prayer I 41, III 227.

bend, *m.i-stem,* [BEND¹]; bond, fetter II 94, III 347.

bēodan, *v.(2),* *w.dat.* BID, command II 53, III 187.

bēon, *inf.* II 47, etc; **bēonne,** *inflected inf.* II 183; **bēo,** *pres. 1 sg. ind.* III 277, *subj.* III 34, *pres. 2 sg. subj.* II 47, *imp. 2 sg.* II 20; **bēoð,** *pres.pl. ind.* II 184, etc; **bist,** *pres. 2 sg.ind.* III 303; **bið,** *pres. 3 sg.ind.* I 222, etc; **eom,** *pres. 1 sg. ind.* I 209; etc; **eart,** *pres. 2 sg. ind.* II 19, etc; **is,** *pres. 3 sg. ind.* I 32, etc; **sȳ,** *pres.subj. 2 sg.* III 315, *3 sg.* I 236, etc; **synd,** II 56, etc, **syndon,** III 337, *pres.pl.*; *anom.v.* BE, am, art, etc; see also **nis.**

gebēor, *m.a-stem,* companion at a feast, feaster I 186, 187, etc.

gebeorgan, *v.(3),w.dat.*[BERGH]; save II 62.

beorht, *adj.* BRIGHT III 211.

beorhte, *adv.* BRIGHT; clearly III 231.

gebēorscype, *m.i-stem,* festivity III 261.

bēotlīc, *adj.* threatening, arrogant II 39.

beran, *v.(4),* BEAR¹; carry I 74, 158, III 245n, 249, etc.

berstan, *v.(3),* *w.dat.* BURST; escape II 51.

besārgian, *w.v.(2),* mourn III 210, 257, 272; regret II 188.

besēon, *v.(5),* [BESEE]; *beseon to,* look at II 54.

besettan, *w.v.(1c),* BESET; cover II 100n.

bestalcian, *w.v.(2),* STALK¹; creep stealthily II 36n.

bestelan, *v.(4),* [BESTEAL]; steal III 347.

beswīcan, *v.(1),* [BESWIKE]; delude III 365.

beswingan, *v.(3),* [BESWINGE]; flog III 140.

gebētan, *w.v.(1b),* [BEET]; make amends I 206, III 217.

betǣcan, *w.v.(1c),* [BETEACH]; commend I 133.

betēon, *v.(2),* *(orig. (1))*, accuse III 220.

betwux, *prep.w.dat.* BETWIXT; between III 13; among I 66, II 20; during II 96; *betwux þam,* meanwhile I 6; **betwux þam þe,** *conj.* while II 104.

beðencan, *w.v.(1c),* [BETHINK]; reflect III 66.

beweaxan, *v.(7),* [BE- + WAX¹]; grow over I 30.

bewerian, *w.v.(2),* *(orig. (1a))*, [BE- + WERE]; protect II 123.

bewestan, *prep.w.dat.* [BEWEST]; to the west of III 15.

bewitan; bewiste, *pret. 3 sg.* I 76, II 130; *pret.pres.(1),* [BIWIT]; look after.

biddan, *v.(5),* *w.acc. of person of whom, (reflex.)dat. of person for whom, gen. of thing requested or dep. clause,* [BID]; ask I 16, III 85, 252, etc; *biddan æt,* ask of III 163; *biddan for,* pray for III 258, 310*.

gebiddan, *v.(5),* *w.reflex.acc. or prep.for,* [I-BID]; pray I 96, 132, etc.

bifian, *w.v.(2),* [BIVE]; tremble III 104.

gebīgan, *w.v.(1b),* [BEY]; bend III 80, 85; convert I 38, 59, 107; translate I 56.

biggeng, *m.i-stem,* [BIGENG]; worship II 70.

GLOSSARY

bigwist, *f.i-stem,* [BEWISTE]; food I 227.

bileafe, see **belǣfan.**

bilewit, *adj.* [BILEWHIT]; innocent II 38.

(ge)bindan, *v.(3),* BIND I 181, 184, etc.

binnan, binnon III 122; *prep. w.dat.* [BIN]; within, in I 8, 118, 144, etc.

bisc(e)op, *m.a-stem,* BISHOP I 44, 56, 58, etc.

bisceopstōl, *m.a-stem,* [BISHOP-STOOL]; cathedral III 15; cathedral town I 112.

bletsian, *w.v.(2),* BLESS¹ I 84n, III 75n; *w.reflex.acc.* cross oneself III 340.

blind, *adj.* BLIND III 130, 134, etc; *as sb.* III 172.

blissian, *w.v.(2),* [BLISS]; rejoice I 188.

blīðe, *adj.* BLITHE; joyful I 54; rejoicing I 181, etc; making merry I 186.

blīðelīce, *adv.* BLITHELY; joyfully II 76, III 306.

blōd, *n.a-stem,* BLOOD II 75, III 223.

geblōwen, *adj.(p.pt.),* BLOWN²; flowering III 292.

blyss, *f.ō-stem,* BLISS; joy I 83.

bōc, *f.athem.stem,* BOOK I 224, II 8, 9, etc.

boda, *m.n-stem,* [BODE¹]; messenger III 49.

bodian, *w.v.(2),* BODE¹; preach I 58, 65, 105.

bodig, *n.a-stem,* BODY II 116, 138.

bodung, *f.ō-stem,* [BODING]; preaching I 54.

gebolgen, *adj.(p.pt.),* [BOL-GHEN]; angry III 171.

bōt, *f.ō-stem,* [BOOT¹]; remedy I 164.

brād, *adj.* BROAD III 80.

brēmel, *m.a-stem,* BRAMBLE II 111, 121.

(ge)bringan, *w.v.(1c),* [I-BRINGE]; BRING I 148, II 167, 177, etc.

broc, *n.a-stem,* BROKE; disease I 181, III 92, 264.

(ge)brocian, *w.v.(2),* afflict I 28, 177.

brosnung, *f.ō-stem,* corruption I 84*, 142.

brōðor, *m.r-stem,* BROTHER I 137, 138, etc; *gebroðrum, dat.pl.* III 203.

brūcan, *v.(2),* *w.gen.* [BROOK]; enjoy II 58, III 211.

(ge)būgan, *v.(2),* BOW¹; submit II 53, 62, 80, etc; retire III 73.

burh, *f.athem.stem,* [BOROUGH]; town I 116; *þa b. Dorcanceaster,* the town of D. I 113.

būtan, būton, [BOUT¹, BUT]; *prep.w.dat.* without I 142, II 114, etc; except I 191, etc; *conj.* except III 15, 304, etc; but that III 197; unless II 61, 79, etc.

byld(o), *f.īn-stem,* [BIELD]; resolution II 84.

byrgen, *f.jō-stem,* [BURIAN]; grave III 33, 37, etc.

gebyrian, *w.v.(1a),* [I-BURE]; be proper II 184, III 261, 262.

byrst, *f.i- or jō-stem,* [BRUST, BIRSE¹]; *BRISTLE* II 100.

bysig, *adj.* BUSY III 196.

bysmor, *m. f. or n. a-stem,* [BISMER]; *to bysmore tucian, tawian,* (ill-)treat humiliatingly, humiliate II 38, 56.

bysmorful(l), *adj.* [BISMER + -FUL]; shameful II 17.

gebysmrian, *w.v.(2),* [BISMER]; humiliate II 91.

gebysnian, *w.v.(2)*, *w.dat.* [BYSEN]; set an example I 60, II 76.

g e b y s n u n g , *f.ō-stem*, [*BYSENING*]; example; *pl.w.sg.meaning* II 89.

C

canones, *Latin nom.pl.* canons, ecclesiastical laws II 182.

cēne, *adj.* KEEN; brave II 43, 63.

cēnlīce, *adv.* KEENLY; bravely I 12.

ceorfan, *v.(3)*, CARVE; cut II 160.

ceorl, *m.a-stem*, CHURL; man III 79, 90.

ceorung, *f.ō-stem*, grumbling III 201.

(ge)cēosan, *v.(2)*, [I-CHEOSE]; CHOOSE II 184, III 383.

cēpan, *w.v.(1b)*, KEEP; *w.gen.* seize II 85; *intrans.* regulate one's conduct III 336.

(ge)cīgan, *w.v.(1b)*, call I 8.

cild, *n.a-stem*, (*orig.s-stem*), CHILD II 37.

clāð, *m.a-stem*, CLOTH I 184.

clǽne, *adj.* CLEAN; unblemished II 148; chaste II 157, 212; innocent II 75.

clypian, *w.v.(2)*, [*CLEPE*]; cry (out), call (out) I 15, 83, etc; call upon II 98, 103; summon I 203, II 49; utter II 179.

clypung, *f.ō-stem*, [*CLEPING*]; shouting II 129n.

cnapa, *m.n-stem*, [KNAPE; *KNAVE*]; boy I 230, III 132, 135.

cnēo(w), *n.wa-stem*, KNEE III 85, 246.

cniht, *m.a-stem*, [KNIGHT]; youth, servant III 152, 268, etc.

coðu, *f.ō-stem*, [COTHE]; disease I 161.

cræft, *m.i-stem*, CRAFT[1]; contrivance II 167.

crēopan, *v.(2)*, CREEP; go haltingly; *w.reflex.dat.pron.* III 84.

crēopere, *m.ja-stem*, [CREEPER]; cripple III 360.

cricc, *f.jō-stem*, CRUTCH III 83, 360.

c r i s t e n , *adj.* [CHRISTEN]; *CHRISTIAN* III 312; *as sb.* I 130, II 38.

cristendōm, *m.a-stem*, CHRISTENDOM; Christianity III 2, 371.

cucu, *adj.* QUICK; alive II 47, 61, 148.

cuman, *v.(4)*, COME I 11, 77, 128, II 60, 167n, 210, III 287, etc.

cunnan; canst, *pres. 2 sg.* III 22; **cūðe, -on,** *pret.* I 55, III 8, etc; **cūð,** *p.pt.* II 219, etc; *pret.pres.(3)*, [CAN[1], CON[1]]; know.

cunnian, *w.v.(2)*, [CUN]; try (to discover) II 167.

cwalu, *f.ō-stem*, [QUALE[1]]; death III 310.

gecwēmednys(s), *f.jō-stem*, [QUEME *v.* + -ED[1] + -NESS]; pleasure III 385*n.

cwēn, *f.i-stem*, QUEEN I 147.

cweðan, *v.(5)*, [QUETHE]; say I 83n, 199, III 14, 136, 317, etc.

gecweðan, *v.(5)*, [I-QUETHE]; say I 143; utter III 94.

(ge)cwȳsan, *w.v.(1b)*, crush III 269.

cyme, *m.i-stem*, [COME]; coming I 49.

cynedōm, *m.a-stem*, [KINDOM]; *KINGDOM* I 120.

cynelīc, *adj.* [KIN[1] + LY[1]]; *KINGLY*; regal I 74.

GLOSSARY

cynelīce, *adv.* [KIN[1] + LY[2]]; *KINGLY*; regally II 55.

cynerīce, *n.ja-stem,* [KINRICK, *KINGRICK*]; kingdom I 87, III 372.

cynin(c)g, kyninge, *dat.sg.* I 101, **cynegas,** *n.pl.* I 111 n; *m.a-stem,* KING I 2, 7, 19, etc.

cȳpin(c)g, *f.ō-stem,* [*CHEAPING*]; marketing, market-place III 62.

cyrce, *f.n-stem,* CHURCH I 35, etc.

cyrcwerd, *m.a-stem,* [CHURCH-WARD]; sacristan III 135.

gecyrran, *w.v.(1b),* [*I-CHERRE*]; turn I 207.

gecyrrednys(s), *f.jō-stem,* conversion I 111.

cystig, *adj.* munificent I 70, II 21.

cȳðan, *w.v.(1b),* [KITHE]; make known III 5; proclaim II 155; tell III 65, etc.

D

dagian, *w.v.(2),* [DAW[1]]; begin to grow light III 102, 143.

dǣd, *f.i-stem,* DEED I 206; action I 122, etc.

dæg, *m.a-stem,* DAY II 2, 124, etc; *anes dæges,* on one and the same day III 159, 376; *sume dæg, instr.sg.* one day III 170.

dæghwāmlīce, *adv.* daily III 201.

dǣl, *m.i-stem,* DEAL[1]; share I 81; portion I 30.

dǣlan, *w.v.(1b),* DEAL; share II 45; give I 48.

dēad, *adj.* DEAD III 242, 255, 259; *as sb.* III 257.

dēaf, *adj.* DEAF III 158.

dearr; dorste, *pret. 3 sg.* II 132, etc; *pret.pres. (3),* DARE[1].

dēað, *m.a-stem,* DEATH I 205, II 181, etc.

gedelf, *n.a-stem,* [DELF[1]]; digging II 176.

deofol, *m.(in sg.) and n.(in pl.)* *a-stem,* (the) DEVIL I 165n, II 28, III 338, 342, etc.

dēor, *n.a-stem,* [DEER]; wild animal II 123, 132.

dēorwurð, *adj.* [DEARWORTH]; precious I 185, III 45.

derian, *w.v.(2), (orig. (1a)), w.dat.* [DERE]; harm III 308, 340.

dīgel, dīg(e)le, *adj.* [DIGHEL]; hidden II 46.

gedihtan, *w.v.(1b),* [DIGHT]; write I 224.

disc, *m.a-stem,* DISH I 75, 79, 80.

dohtor, *f.r-stem,* DAUGHTER I 147.

dōm, *m.a-stem,* DOOM II 208; judgement II 188.

(ge)dōn, *anom.v.* [I-DO]; DO I 81, 182, II 104, etc; act III 255; carry out III 71; cause III 313; put I 167, III 222, 310; *up (ge)don,* exhume III 113, 115 f.

(ge)dreccan, *w.v.(1c),* [DRETCH[1]]; afflict I 165.

Drihten, *m.a-stem,* [DRIGHTIN]; (the) Lord, God I 122, II 186, 214, etc.

drincan, *v.(3),* DRINK III 259, 314.

drohtnung, *f.ō-stem,* mode of life I 45n, III 9.

dumb, *adj.* DUMB III 132, 134, 158.

duru, *f.u-stem,* DOOR II 169.

dūst, *n.a-stem,* DUST[1]; earth I 164, 184, 187, etc.

gedwimor, *n.a-stem,* illusion, deception III 339.

93

dwollīce, *adv.* [*DWALE adj.* + -LY²]; misguidedly, foolishly III 255.

ģedwyld, *n.i-stem,* [DWILD]; error, foolishness I 150, II 203.

dȳre, *adj. DEAR¹;* precious III 45.

dyrstiglīce, *adv.* presumptuously III 252.

dysig, *adj.* [DIZZY]; foolish III 242.

dyslīc, *adj.* foolish I 202, III 252.

dyslīce, *adv.* [*DIZZILY*]; foolishly III 248.

E

ēac, *adv.* [EKE]; also I 85, 100, 183, etc; *eac swilce,* likewise, also I 26, 166, etc.

ēadig, *adj.* [EADI]; blessed I 11, II 14, 216, III 186.

ģeēadmēdan, *w.v.(1b),* humble III 76 n.

ēadmōd, *adj.* [EDMOD]; humble I 70, II 16, III 76.

ēaģe, *n.n-stem,* EYE¹ III 93, etc.

ēahhring, *m.a-stem,* [EYE¹ + RING]; eyesocket III 232 n.

eahta, eahte, II 165n, III 13n; *num.* EIGHT I 124, III 110, etc.

eahtatȳne, *num.* EIGHTEEN III 122.

ēalā, *interj.* O II 55, III 54, etc.

eald, *adj.* OLD III 28, 281, 359.

eall, *adj.* ALL I 19, 45, 218n, etc; *adv.* entirely I 190, 208, etc; *ealles to swyðe,* all too much III 336; *mid ealle,* completely I 79, III 233*n; *geond eall,* everywhere I 71.

eallswā, *adv.* AS; *eallswa . . . swilce,* just as . . . as if II 148.

eallunga, *adv.* [ALLINGE]; entirely II 222.

Eallwealdend, *m.nd-stem,* [ALL-WIELDING]; ruler of all I 21.

ealmihtig, see ælmihtig.

ēam, *m.a-stem,* [EME]; uncle I 6.

eard, *m.a-stem,* [ERD]; native land I 211, II 58, 69, III 166.

ēare, *n.n-stem,* EAR¹ III 222.

earfoðlīce, *adv.* [ARVETH-LICHE]; with difficulty III 93, 131.

earhlīce, *adv.* [ARGHLY]; fearfully III 53.

earm, *m.a-stem,* ARM¹ I 28, 136, 143, III 269.

earm, *adj.* [ARM]; unfortunate, unhappy II 56, 222, III 79, 142.

earming, *m.a-stem,* [ARMING]; wretch III 367.

earmlīc, *adj.* [ARMLICH]; wretched I 205.

earmlīce, *adv.* [ARMLICHE]; wretchedly II 171, 197.

ģeearnian, *w.v.(2),* EARN¹, merit I 232, III 358; obtain by merit III 227.

ģeearnung, *f.ō-stem,* EARNING; merit I 32*n, etc; meriting I 194.

ēast, *adv.* EAST, eastwards II 31.

Ēasterdæg, *m.a-stem,* EASTER-DAY I 74.

ēaðe, *adv.* [EATH]; easily III 126.

ēaðelīce, *adv.* [EATHLY]; easily III 57.

ēce, *adj.* [ECHE]; eternal I 228, 232, II 155, III 43.

ēcnys(s), *f.jō-stem,* [ECHENESS]; *on ecnysse,* eternally I 36, 236, III 388.

ģeefenlǣcan, *w.v.(1b),* w.dat. [EVENLECHE]; imitate II 89n, III 309.

efsian, *w.v.(2)* [EVESE]; cut the hair of II 159.

efstan, *w.v.(1b),* hasten III 43.

eft, *adv.* [EFT]; afterwards I 117, 147, etc; again I 51, 229, etc.

egeful, *adj.* AWFUL, terrifying III 342.

egeslīc, *adj.* [EISLICH]; dreadful I 181.

egeslīce, *adv.* [EISLICHE]; dreadfully III 79.

geegsian, *w.v.*(*2*), [EISIE]; terrify III 62.

embe, *prep.w.acc.* [EMBE, UMBE]; round II 150; about, concerning I 37, 201; *to beonne embe,* to concern oneself with II 183; *embe lang,* after a long time I 172 f.

geemtigian, *w.v.*(*2*), EMPTY, put out, remove III 233n.

ende, *m.ja-stem,* END II 189, *228,* III 360, 367; point of death I 203.

endebyrdnys(s), *f.jō-stem,* order III 68.

endemes, *adv.* together, in a body III 189; with one accord II 120, III 195.

geendian, *w.v.*(*2*), [YEND]; END[1], die I 205, II 197.

geendung, *f.ō-stem,* [YEND *v.* + -ING[1]]; ENDING I 132.

engel, *m.a-stem,* ANGEL I 230n, III 175.

(ge)ēode, -on, see **(ge)gān.**

eorðe, *f.n-stem,* EARTH[1], soil I 163, 167; ground I 171, II 54, 208; (this) world II 227.

eorðfæst, *adj.* [EARTHFAST]; rooted in the ground II 93.

ēow, see **gē.**

ēower, *adj.* YOUR I 211, III 245.

ercestōl, *m.a-stem,* [ARCH- + STOOL]; (cathedral containing) archbishop's throne III 382.

F

faran, *v.*(*6*), FARE[1], go I 206, II 77, III 31, 288, 289.

faru, *f.ō-stem,* [FARE[1]]; journey III 155.

fæder, *m.r-stem,* FATHER II 22, 228.

fægen, *adj.* FAIN; glad III 289; *w.gen.* glad of I 111.

fæger, *adj.* FAIR III 325.

fægnian, *w.v.*(*2*), [FAIN]; rejoice III 83; *w.gen.* rejoice in I 50, etc.

fægre, *adv.* FAIR; beautifully III 292.

færlīc, *adj.* [FERLY]; sudden II 52.

færlīce, *adv.* [FERLY]; suddenly I 190, II 36, etc; immediately III 144, etc.

fæstan, *w.v.*(*1b*), FAST[2] II 190n.

fæste, *adv.* FAST II 177, III 60.

fæsten, *n.ja-stem,* [FASTEN]; fasting II 159, III 217.

(ge)fæstnian, *w.v.*(*2*), FASTEN I 138.

feallan, *v.*(*7*), FALL I 27, 170, etc; fall slain I 130, 132, etc; kneel I 16, 19.

feawa, *adj.pl.* FEW II 9; uninflected, III 127; as *sb.w.part. gen.* III 120.

fec, *n.a-stem,* [FEC]; space of time III 130n.

(ge)feccan, fette, *pret. 3 sg.* I 29; *w.v.*(*3*), FETCH; obtain I 196, III 81.

fēdan, *w.v.*(*1b*), FEED III 313.

fela, *indeclinable sb.* (*w.gen.*) *or adj.* [FELE]; many I 26, 160, etc.

feld, *m.u-stem,* FIELD I 169, etc.

gefeoht, *n.a-stem,* FIGHT, battle I 21, 129, etc.

feohtan, *v.*(*3*), FIGHT II 60.

fēole, *f.n-stem,* FILE[1] II 169.

fēolian, *w.v.*(*2*), file II 169.

fēond, *m.nd-stem,* [FIEND]; enemy I 13, 17, 22, III 311n, 312.

feorh, *n.a-stem*, life II 41, 61.

fēower, *num.* FOUR I 88, etc.

gefēra, *m.n-stem*, [YFERE]; companion I 5, 15, 63, II 126.

fēran, *w.v.(1b)*, [FERE¹]; go I 3, 58, 65, etc; fare II 171.

ferian, *w.v.(2)*, (*orig.* (*1a*)), [FERRY]; carry I 117, 140, etc.

feter, *f.ō-stem*, FETTER III 346, 349.

fette, see **(ge)feccan.**

fīf, *num.* FIVE III 120, 121, etc.

findan, *v.(3)*, FIND III 6, 45, 128.

flǣsc, *n.i-stem*, FLESH I 142.

flēam, *m.a-stem*, [FLEME²]; flight II 61, 67.

flēogan, *v.(2)*, FLY¹ III 290.

flēon, *v.(2)*, FLEE I 191.

flocc, *m.a-stem*, FLOCK¹; company III 154.

flota, *m.n-stem*, [FLOTE¹]; fleet II 27.

flothere, *m.ja-stem*, [FLOAT *sb.* + HERE]; seaborne (pirate) force II 110.

flotman, *m.athem.stem*, [FLOAT *sb.* + MAN¹]; pirate II 60, 66, 101, 117.

folc, *n.a-stem*, FOLK; (common) people I 65, etc; nation I 128, etc; subjects I 50, 123, etc.

ₒolclīc, *adj.* [FOLK + LY¹]; popular II 204; universal II 146.

folgere, *m.ja-stem*, FOLLOWER III 311.

folgian, *w.v.(2)*, *w.dat.* FOLLOW II 75, 135; yield to III 38; be guided by III 343n.

fōn, *v.(7)*, [FANG¹]; *feng to rice*, succeeded to the throne I 137; *fengon togædere*, joined together II 143, (in battle) I 129.

for, *prep.w.dat.(instr.)*, FOR I 22, 90, 93, etc; on account of III 24, 70, etc; in the eyes of I 121, II 192, etc; *w.acc.* for I 132,

III 310*, etc; **for þan (þam) þe,** *conj.* because I 55, 226, II 75, 98, etc.

forbærnan, *w.v.(1b)*, [FORBURN]; burn I 195.

forbēodan, *v.(2)*, *w.dat.* FORBID II 89, 182, III 343n.

forbyrnan, *v.(3)*, [FORBURN]; burn I 191n.

forceorfan, *v.(3)*, [FORCARVE]; cut off III 222.

forealdian, *w.v.(2)*, [FOROLD]; become infirm with age II 7.

forescēawian, *w.v.(2)*, [FORESHOW]; ordain II 77.

foresecgan, *w.v.(3)*, [FORESAY]; mention earlier I 29, 141, etc.

forgifan, *v.(5)*, *w.acc. and dat.* [FORGIVE]; grant II 142, III 96, 234, etc.

forgifnys(s), *f.jō-stem*, FORGIVENESS III 253.

forhæfednys(s), *f.jō-stem*, [FORHEVEDNESS]; continence I 62.

forhelan, *v.(4)*, [FORHELE]; conceal III 67n.

forhtian, *w.v.(2)*, [FRIGHT]; be afraid II 51.

forhwega, *adv.* somewhere II 119.

forlǣtan, *v.(7)*, [FORLET¹]; abandon III 172, 195; leave III 176.

forliger, *n.a-stem*, unchastity II 156.

forma, *adj.* [FORME]; first III 38.

foroft, *adv.* [FOR-¹ + OFT]; very often III 219.

forpǣran, *w.v.(1b)*, bring disaster upon III 339.

forraðe, *adv.* [FOR-¹ + RATHE]; very soon III 332n.

forrǣdan, *w.v.(1b)*, [FORREDE]; plot against, deprive unjustly or treacherously III 339.

forrotian, *w.v.(2)*, [FORROT]; decay I 84.

forsacan, *v.(6)*, FORSAKE; reject I 158.

forsēon, *v.(5)*, [FORSEE]; scorn, neglect II 86, III 216*.

forslēan, *v.(6)*, [FOR-¹ + SLAY¹]; cut through II 149.

forð, *adv.* FORTH I 176; *forð mid*, along with I 185, II 135; *forð on*, [FORTHON]; continually III 197; see also **tēon**.

forðearle, *adv.* greatly I 29.

forōfēran, *w.v.(1b)*, [FORTH + FERE¹]; depart, die II 4.

fōt, *m.athem.stem*, FOOT I 66, 182, II 130; III 59, 105, etc.

fōtcops, *m.a-stem*, [FOOT + COPS]; fetter III 144.

fracod, *adj.* [FRAKED]; vile, wicked I 206.

fram, *prep.w.dat.* FROM I 3, 46, 100, etc; (cured) of I 161, 180; by I 7, II 66.

gefremian, *w.v.(2)*, (*orig.* (*1a*)), III 118, 355, 378; gefremman, *w.v.(1a)*, I 105, II 173; [FREME]; perform, commit.

gefrēogan, *w.v.(2)*, [Y-FREE]; FREE III 147.

frēond, *m.nd-stem*, FRIEND I 3, 196, III 95n, 152.

gefri(g)nan, *v.(1)*, (*orig.*(*3*)), [FRAYNE]; learn III 164*n.

fruma, *m.n-stem*, [FRUME]; *æt fruman*, at first III 66.

fūl, *adj.* FOUL II 74n.

ful(l), *adj.* FULL; whole III 169.

ful(l), *adv.* FULL; perfectly, very II 63, 118, III 326.

(ge)fullian, *w.v.(2)*, [FULL¹]; baptize I 5*.

fullīce, *adv.* FULLY II 190, III 164.

fulluht, *n.i-stem*, [FULLOUGHT]; baptism I 111n, etc.

fūlnys(s), *f.jō-stem*, disgusting behaviour III 256.

fultum, *m.a-stem*, [FULTUM]; aid II 98; forces II 60.

fulwyrcan, *w.v.(1c)*, [FULL + WORK]; complete I 91.

fundian, *w.v.(2)*, [FOUND¹]; direct one's course I 185.

fūs, *adj.* [FOUS]; hastening II 82.

fyll, *m.i-stem*, FALL, death (in battle) I 10, 134.

gefyllan, *w.v.(1b)*, [FILL]; fulfill I 141.

fylst, *m.* [FILST]; assistance III 287.

(ge)fylstan, *w.v.(1b)*, *w.dat.* [FILST]; assist I 13, 127.

fȳr, *n.a-stem*, FIRE I 188, etc.

fyrd, *f.i-stem*, [FERD¹]; army II 44, 82.

fyrlen, *adj.* distant I 106.

fyrmest, *sup.adj.* FOREMOST II 27, III 154.

gefyrn, *adv.* [FERN]; some while ago, previously I 182, III 26.

fyrst, *m.i-stem*, [FRIST]; space of time II 112; respite I 209; *on fyrste*, after a time II 141; *to langum fyrste*, for a long time I 115.

fyrst, *sup.adj.* FIRST; foremost II 27.

gefyrōrian, *w.v.(2)*, FURTHER; advance III 372.

G

gafeluc, *m.a-stem*, [GAVELOCK]; javelin II 99.

gegafspræc, *f.jō-stem*, [GAFF *sb.*² + SPEECH¹]; scurrilous talk, buffoonery III 261n.

galga, *m.n-stem*, GALLOWS II 178.

gamen, *n.a-stem*, GAME, amusement II 99.

gān, ēode, -on, *pret.* I 20, 63, 75, etc; *anom.v.* GO II 125.

gegān, *anom.v.* [I-GO]; *him geeode þæt,* it befell him that I 85.

gangan, *v.*(7), [GANG¹]; go III 199; *w.reflex.dat.* III 37; walk I 182n.

gāst, *m.a-stem,* GHOST, spirit II 229.

ge, *nom.* III 244, etc; **ēow,** *acc.* II 77, *dat.* III 246, 285; *pron.* YE, YOU.

ge, *conj.* [YE]; *ge . . . ge,* both . . . and II 183, 200, etc.

gēar, *n.a-stem,* YEAR I 8, 124n, etc.

geare, *adv.* [YARE]; well I 18.

gēomerung, *f.ō-stem,* [YOMER *v.* + -ING¹]; moaning, lamentation II 187, III 275, 349.

geond, *prep.w.acc.* [YOND]; through, throughout I 58, 77, etc; during, for III 119, 130.

georne, *adv.* [YERNE]; earnestly I 63, II 189, III 64, 259.

geornfulnys(s), *f.jō-stem,* [YEARNFULNESS]; zeal I 72.

geornlīce, *adv.* [YERNLY]; diligently III 107; fervently III 155.

gif, *conj.* IF I 207, 211, 214, 222, etc; whether III 373; to see whether II 121.

gifan, *v.*(5), *w.acc. and dat.* GIVE I 111.

gifu, *f.ō-stem,* [GIVE¹]; gift I 47, II 163.

gīt, *adv.* YET III 50; still I 119, 230; see also **þagīt.**

(ge)glencgan, *w.v.*(1b), adorn III 21, 198.

God, *m.a-stem,* GOD I 3, 14, etc.

gōd, good, III 326; *adj.* GOOD I 207, III 199n, etc; *neut.sg. as sb.* good thing III 384; *pl. as sb.* good men III 78, 340.

gegōdian, *w.v.*(2), [GOOD]; endow II 164*.

gōdnys(s), *f.jō-stem,* GOODNESS I 229.

gold, *n.a-stem,* GOLD¹ II 163, III 46, 293.

goldhord, *m.a-stem,* GOLD-HOARD; treasure II 46, III 45.

grǣdig, *adj.* GREEDY; voracious II 131.

grǣg, GREY II 129n.

gremian, *w.v.*(2), (*orig.* (1a)), [GREME]; anger III 260.

grymetian, *w.v.*(2), **grymettan,** *w.v.*(1b), roar II 197*n.

gylt, *m.i-stem,* GUILT; offence III 139, 352.

gȳman, *w.v.*(1b), [YEME]; heed, act in accordance with I 200.

gȳmelēast, *f.ō-stem,* [YEME-LEST]; negligence III 7, 346.

gymstān, *m.a-stem,* GEMSTONE; jewel III 293.

gyrnan, *w.v.*(1b), YEARN for; desire, request III 247.

H

habban, *w.v.*(3), HAVE I 212, 213, 228, etc; *as (plu)perf.aux.* I 92, 176, etc; take II 117.

(ge)hādian, *w.v.*(2), [HADE¹]; **gehādod,** *p.pt. as sb.* cleric II 182.

(ge)hāl, *adj.* [Y-HOLE]; WHOLE, HALE; sound, in good health I 175, 214, etc; uncorrupted I 142, etc; unimpaired III 168, 233.

hālga, *m.n-stem,* [HALLOW¹]; saint III 67, 71, 89, etc.

(ge)hālian, *w.v.*(2), heal II 149.

hālig, *adj.* HOLY I 62, 74, 184, etc; saintly I 231, 233, etc.

hāligdōm, *m.a-stem,* [HALI-DOM]; relic(s) II 161.

hālsian, *w.v.(2),* [HALSE¹]; entreat III 29.

hām, *adv.* HOME II 11, 134, etc.

hāmfæst, *adj.* resident III 29.

hand, *f.u-stem,* HAND I 82, 139, etc.

handbred, *n.a-stem,* [HAND-BREDE]; palm (of the hand) I 99.

hangian, *w.v.(2),* HANG II 175, III 233.

hātan, hēt, *pres.ind. 3 sg.* II 45n, III 31n; *v.(7),* [HIGHT¹]; command I 8on, etc; **hātte,** *pass. 3 sg. (orig.pres.),* was named II 4; **gehāten,** *p.pt* named I 2, 32, etc.

gehæft, *adj.(p.pt.),* imprisoned III 138, 356*n.

hæftnēd, *f.i-stem,* [+ NEED]; custody; *pl.w.sg.meaning* III 139.

gehǣlan, *w.v.(1),* HEAL¹, cure I 26, 31, 225*, etc.

Hǣlend, *m.nd-stem,* [HEALEND]; Saviour II 79, 88, 96, etc.

hǣl(o), *f.īn-stem,* [HEAL]; healing, cure III 85, 96, 101, etc.

hæpse, *f.n-stem,* HASP, bolt II 168.

hærlīce, see **heardlīce.**

hǣs, *f.i-stem,* HEST; behest II 85n, III 51, 67.

hǣðen, *adj.* HEATHEN I 102, 135, etc; *as sb.* I 105, 130, etc.

he, *nom.sg.m.* I 15, etc; **hine,** *acc.sg.m.* I 12, etc; **his,** *gen. sg.m.* I 5, etc; **him,** *dat.sg.m.* I 5, etc, *neut.* II 129, etc, *plur.* I 60, etc; **hēo,** *nom.sg.f.* I 149, etc; **hi,** *acc.sg.f.* III 142, etc, *nom.pl.* I 19, etc, *acc.pl.* I 89, etc; **hire,** *gen.sg.f.* II 216, etc, *dat.sg.f.* III 144; **hit,** *nom.sg.n.* I 52, etc, *acc.sg.n.* I 204, etc; **heora,** *gen.pl.* I 80, etc;

heom, *dat.pl.* I 22, etc; *pron.* HE, SHE, IT, etc; *referring to sb. of different gender,* I 179n, II 10n; *reflex.* I 96, III 252, 340, etc; *pleonastic reflex.dat.* III 32n, 37n, etc; *possessive dat.* II 106n, etc.

hēafod, *n.a-stem,* HEAD II 106, 114, 126, 131, etc.

hēafodbend, *m.i-stem,* [HEAD + BEND¹]; headband III 352.

hēafodman, *m.athem.stem,* HEADMAN, leader II 28; ruler II 19.

hēah, *adj.* HIGH I 187, II 178.

(ge)healdan, *v.(7),* [I-HALD]; HOLD; keep I 94, etc; keep safe II 132, etc; rule over I 120; maintain III 217.

healf, *f.ō-stem,* HALF; side II 18.

healf, *adj.* HALF; *hi healfe,* half of them III 362.

hēalīc, *adj.* [HIGHLY]; high III 76; of great splendour I 154.

heall, *f.ō-stem,* HALL; royal residence II 87.

healt, *adj.* HALT, lame III 158.

hēap, *m.a-stem,* HEAP; company III 128.

heard, *adj.* HARD; cruel II 94.

heardlīce, hærlīce, II 46(?); *adv.* HARDLY; boldly, fiercely II 42, 81(?); swiftly (?) II 46.

hefegian, *w.v.(2),* [HEAVY]; weigh down, afflict III 88.

hefig, *adj.* HEAVY¹; grave III 352.

hell, *f.jō-stem,* HELL I 206.

(ge)helpan, *v.(3),* *w.gen. or dat.* HELP I 226, III 142, 274n, etc.

gehende, *adj.* [HEND]; close at hand, II 50, 107.

heofon, *m.a-stem,* HEAVEN; *pl.w.sg.meaning* I 99*n, 153, etc.

99

heofone, *f.n-stem,* HEAVEN I 93.
heofonlĭc, *adj.* HEAVENLY I 152*n, II 153, 228.
heonon, *adv.* [HEN]; HENCE III 26.
heononforð, *adv.* [HENFORTH]; henceforth III 297.
heorte, *f.n-stem,* HEART I 46, 219, III 173, etc.
hĕr, *adv.* HERE I 141, II 44, etc.
hĕræfter, *adv.* HEREAFTER II 10.
here, *m.ja-stem,* [HERE]; army II 85.
heretoga, *m.n-stem,* [HERE-TOGA]; commander II 79.
hergian, *w.v.*(2), HARROW, HARRY, devastate II 26.
hergung, *f.ō-stem,* HARROWING, HARRYING, raid II 141.
herian, *w.v.*(1a), [HERY]; praise III 189, 202, 280.
hetelĭce, *adv.* [HATELY]; violently III 139.
hihtan, *w.v.*(1b), [HIGHT²]; trust III 78.
hingrian, *w.v.*(2), (*orig.* (1b)), *impers.w.dat.* HUNGER III 313.
hlāford, *m.a-stem,* LORD, master I 1on, III 65, etc.
hlǣder, *f.ō-stem,* LADDER II 170, 176.
hlēor, *n.a-stem,* [LEER¹]; cheek III 234.
hlīsa, *m.n-stem,* fame I 197.
hlīsfullĭce, *adv.* gloriously I 120.
hlyd, *n.a-stem,* LID III 56.
hlyst, *m.* or *f.i-stem,* [LIST¹]; hearing III 225, 235.
g e h o f e r o d , *adj.(p.pt.),* [HOVERED]; hump-backed III 79.
hofor, *m.a-stem,* hump III 80, 87.
hogian, *w.v.*(2), (*orig.* (3)), [HOW¹]; think I 94, 201.

holt, *m.* or *n.a-stem,* HOLT¹, wood II 119.
hōn, *v.*(7), HANG II 178.
hoppan, *w.v.*(1b), **hoppian,** *w.v.*(2), HOP III 348n.
hord, *m. a-stem,* HOARD¹; treasure III 45.
hors, *n.a-stem,* HORSE I 170, III 268.
horsbǣr, *f.ō-stem,* [HORSE-BIER]; horse-litter III 151.
hraðe, *adv.* [RATHE]; quickly, immediately, soon I 48, 57, II 77, 195, III 213.
hrǣding, *f.ō-stem,* haste II 139.
hrepian, *w.v.*(2), (*orig.* (1)), [REPE¹]; touch I 174.
hricg, *m.ja-stem,* [RIDGE¹]; back III 87.
hringe, *f.n-stem,* ring III 37, 38, 40, etc.
hū, *adv.* HOW III 6, 172, 285, etc; what III 306, 319; by which III 339.
hund, *num.* [HUND]; hundred III 123.
hundtwelftig, *num.* one hundred and twenty III 263.
hungrig, *adj.* HUNGRY II 131.
hūru, *adv.* [HURE]; at least III 121, 151, 227; especially II 115.
hūs, *n.a-stem,* HOUSE¹ I 186, 190, 191; monastery III 117n.
huxlĭce, *adv.* [HUX + LY²]; ignominiously II 92.
gehwā, *pron.* everyone II 206.
gehwanon, *adv.* [Y- + WHENNE]; from all quarters I 77.
hwǣr, *adv.* WHERE II 126, 226, III 27, 87; *swa hwær swa,* [WHERESO]; where(so)ever I 98.
gehwǣr, *adv.* [Y-WHERE]; everwhere II 120.

hwæt, *pron.* WHAT III 63, 68; *hwæt . . . manna,* what manner of man III 315; *swa hwæt swa* [WHATSO]; what(so)ever I 47.

hwæt, *interj.* WHAT; well, so I 37, 49, 120, etc.

hwæðær, *conj.* WHETHER II 195.

hwī, *adv.* WHY; because III 51.

hwider, *adv.* WHITHER; *swa hwider swa,* [WHITHERSO]; whithersoever I 64 f, 219.

gehwider, *adv.* [Y- +WHITHER]; everywhere III 170.

hwīlon, *adv.* [WHILOM]; sometimes III 121, 193; once III 241, 263, 376.

hwīlwendlīc, *adj.* [WHILWENDLIC]; temporal, transitory I 94.

hwōnlīce, *adv.* [WHON² + -LY²]; but little I 95.

hwylc, *adj.* WHICH; what III 165.

gehwylc, *adj.* many III 382; *pron.w.gen.pl.* EACH I 196.

gehȳran, *w.v.(1b),* [Y-HERE]; HEAR II 108, III 223, 227, etc; hear of II 204; obey III 71.

hyrdræden, *f.jō-stem,* [HERD² + -RED]; care, protection II 133.

hȳred, *m.a-stem,* [HIRD]; household III 215.

hyrne, *f.n-stem,* [HERN]; corner I 163.

gehȳrsumian, *w.v.(2),* *w.dat.* [HEARSUM]; obey III 51.

I

ic, *nom.* I 205, 206, etc; **me,** *acc.* III 176, etc, *dat.* I 212, etc; *pron.* I, ME.

īdel, *adj.* [IDLE]; *on idel,* in vain II 171.

īgel, *m.* [IL]; hedgehog II 100.

īgland, *n.a-stem,* ISLAND III 375.

in(n), *adv.* IN I 75, II 167.

innan, *prep.w.dat.* [INNE]; within II 87, 147.

in(ne)werd, *adj.* INWARD; inmost III 173, 273.

into, *prep.w.dat.* INTO I 159, 234, III 18, 116, 223.

īs, *n.a-stem,* ICE I 28.

īsen, *n.a-stem,* IRON; iron ring III 57.

iugoð, *f.ō-stem,* YOUTH I 3.

iung, *adj.* YOUNG I 62*, II 7.

K

kyning, see **cynin(c)g.**

L

lā, *interj.* LO; O III 35, 315.

lāf, *f.ō-stem,* [LAVE¹]; *to lafe beon,* be left II 113, III 367.

land, *n.a-stem,* LAND II 26, 29, 30, etc.

landfolc, *n.a-stem,* [LANDFOLK]; inhabitants II 113, 162.

landlēoda, *m.i-stem pl.* inhabitants II 137; nation II 56.

lang, *adj.* LONG¹ I 33, 115; *as sb.* a long time I 173.

lange, *adv.* LONG III 379; for a long time I 177, etc.

langlīce, *adv.* [LONG *adj.*¹ + -LY²]; for a long time II 95.

lār, *f.ō-stem,* LORE¹; teaching I 63, 114, II 19, III 324; learning I 200.

lārēow, *m.wa-stem,* [LAREW]; teacher I 41.

lǽttēow, *m.wa-stem,* [LATTEW]; guide III 132, 171, etc.

lāð, *adj.* LOATH; hateful III 347.

lāðian, *w.v.(2),* *w.dat.* LOATHE; become irksome to III 192.

gelæccan, w.v.(rc), [I-LECCHE]; seize III 221.

lǣdan, w.v.(rb), LEAD¹ II 92, 181, III 170, 184; take I 185.

læncg, comp.adv. [LENG]; longer III 211n.

lǣran, w.v.(rb), w.acc. or dat. [LERE]; teach I 61n, III 324.

gelǣred, adj.(p.pt.), [YLERED]; learned I 200, II 1.

lǣs, comp.adv. LESS; þe lǣs þe, conj. LEST I 222, III 343.

gelǣstan, w.v.(rb), [YLAST]; perform III 204.

lǣwede, adj. [LEWD]; lay I 67n.

geleafa, m.n-stem, [YLEVE]; belief, faith I 12, 22, 40, etc.

geleafful, adj. [LEAFFUL]; believing, Christian I 53, etc.

leahtor, m.a-stem, sin II 18.

lecgan, lēdon, pret.pl. II 138, gelēd, p.pt. I 143; w.v.(rc), LAY¹ II 146n.

gelendan, w.v.(rb),[LEND¹]; land II 29.

lēode, lēoda, m.i-stem pl. [LEDE]; people I 10, 38, etc.

lēof, adj. [LIEF]; beloved II 65, III 271; as term of address, II 59; as sb. sir, master III 26, 35, etc; me leofre wǣre, I should prefer II 56 f.

leofað, leofode, etc, see lybban

lēoht, n.a-stem, LIGHT I 153, III 131, 211, 246.

lēohtlīce, adv. LIGHTLY; without trouble or effort, quickly II 139.

leornian, w.v.(2), (orig. (3)), LEARN I 64.

līc, n.a-stem, [LICH]; body I 116, II 114, 152, III 242, etc.

gelīc, adj.w.dat. [YLIKE]; ALIKE; like I 171, II 198.

licgan, v.(5), LIE¹ I 28, 177, II 200, III 276n, etc; licgan on cneowum, kneel III 246n.

līchama, m.n-stem, [LICHAM]; body II 146, 148, etc.

līcrest, f.jō-stem, [LICH sb. + REST¹]; hearse I 151.

līctūn, m.a-stem, [LICH sb. + TOWN]; graveyard III 125.

līf, n.a-stem, LIFE I 44, 131, etc; on life, ALIVE, living I 227, III 8, etc.

lim, n.a-stem, LIMB¹ I 175, 180.

gelimp, n.a-stem, [LIMP¹]; event, disaster II 52.

gelimpan, v.(3), [I-LIMP]; happen I 52, 72, 109, II 25.

līthwōn, adv. [A LITEL WAN (s.v. WHON²)]; but little I 200.

lof, n.a-stem, [LOF]; praise I 114, II 219, III 386.

lofsang, m.a-stem, [LOF-SONG]; song of praise III 137, 192, etc; Lauds III 144.

gelōgian, w.v.(2), deposit, inter I 118; fill II 211*; gelogodon upp, laid up, interred I 159n.

gelōm, adj. frequent II 144 (or adv.), 152, III 380 (or adv.).

gelōme, adv. [YLOME]; often II 127.

losian, w.v.(2), [LOSE]; perish I 222, III 368.

lufian, w.v.(2), LOVE¹ I 61, 95, 149.

lufu, f.ō-stem, LOVE II 70, 160.

lūtan, v.(2), [LOUT¹]; stoop II 176.

lybban, w.v.(3), LIVE I 39, 61, 226*n, II 70, etc.

gelȳfan, w.v.(rb), [YLEVE]; believe I 214, etc; w.dat. III 36, etc; w.clause, III 181, etc; w.prep.on, believe in III 365, etc.

gelȳfed, adj.(p.pt.), believing I 3, 7; pious III 20n.

lyft, f.i-stem, [LIFT¹]; air III 291.

GLOSSARY

lȳtel, *adj.* LITTLE; small I 12, III 139n.
lȳtle, *adv.* LITTLE; shortly III 184.
lȳðre, *adj.* [LITHER]; base III 176.

M

macian, *w.v.(2)*, MAKE; perform II 221; inflict II 153; *macian up*, put up III 362.
magan; mæg, *pres.ind. 1 sg.* III 175, etc, *3 sg.* III 208, etc; **mæge**, *pres.subj. 2 sg.* II 60, etc, *3 sg.* III 344; **mage**, *pres.ind. 1 pl.* III 354, *subj. 2 sg.* II 48; **magon**, *pres. 2 pl.* III 244, *3 pl.* II 213, etc; **miht**, *pres.ind. 2 sg.* III 316; **mihte**, *pret.sg.* I 24, 42, etc; **mihton**, *pret.pl.* II 121, etc; *pret.pres.v.* MAY, might, can, could; *w.inf. of vb. of motion omitted* III 149n, 282.
manega, *adj.pl.* MANY I 195, 234, etc; *as sb.* I 164.
mānful(l), *adj.* [MAN *sb.²* + -FUL]; wicked III 299.
manian, *w.v.(2)*, exhort III 384.
man(n), *m.athem.stem*, MAN¹, person I 26, 27, etc; one III 208, etc; *often forming pass. periphrasis*, I 29, 70, 74, etc.
manrǣden(n), *f.jō-stem*, [MAN-RED]; homage II 40.
manslaga, *m.n-stem*, [MAN-SLAYER]; murderer III 299.
martyr, *m.a-stem*, MARTYR II 203.
māðm, *m.a-stem*, [MADME]; precious thing II 166, III 46.
mǣden, *n.a-stem*, MAIDEN I 177, 179.
mǣg, *m.a-stem*, [MAY²]; kinsman I 4, 92, etc.

mægen, *n.a-stem*, MAIN¹; virtue I 68.
mǣre, *adj.* [MERE¹]; glorious I 35, 44, II 35, etc.
mǣrsian, *w.v.(2)*, glorify III 190, 387.
mǣrð, *f.ō-stem*, glorious deed III 190.
mæsseprēost, *m.a-stem*, MASS-PRIEST, priest I 198, 215.
mæsserēaf, *n.a-stem*, [MASS + REAF]; mass vestments III 294.
mæssian, *w.v.(2)*, [MASS¹]; celebrate mass III 295.
me, see **ic**.
mennisc, *adj.* [MANNISH]; human I 150, II 203.
mēos, *m.a-stem*, [MESE¹]; moss I 30.
mergen, *m.a-stem*, MORN; morning I 20n, 156, etc.
gemētan, *w.v.(1b)*, MEET II 81, III 62; find II 121n, III 108n.
mete, *m.i-stem*, [MEAT]; food III 313.
mettrum, *adj.* sick I 161.
micel, *adj.* [MICKLE; MUCH]; great I 23, 67, II 122, etc; *oð þone micclan dæg*, till Doomsday II 209; **micclum**, *adv.* much, greatly I 149, 156, etc.
mid, *prep.w.dat. and instr.* [MID¹]; with I 12, 49, 60, etc; among III 202, 207; *postponed*, I 5*n, etc; *þe ... mid*, with which I 30, 162; *mid sandum mid ealle*, food and all I 79; **mid þam þe**, *conj.* when II 87, etc; as I 171, etc.
miht, *f.i-stem*, MIGHT; power II 48, III 303; mighty deeds III 9.
mihtig, *adj.* MIGHTY III 174, 181.

103

mihtiglīce, *adv.* MIGHTILY, by might III 387.

milde, *adj.* MILD; merciful III 179.

mildheort, *adj.* [MILDHEART]; merciful II 179.

gemiltsian, *w.v.*(2), *w.dat.* [I-MILCE]; have mercy on I 134, III 176.

mīn, *adj.* MINE; MY I 208, II 57, etc.

mislīc, *adj.* [MISLICH]; various I 161.

mislīce, *adv.* [MISLICHE]; variously III 156, 263.

mōd, *n.a-stem,* [MOOD¹]; heart I 49, II 115; *mid mode,* heartily II 64.

mōdig, *adj.* [MOODY]; proud I 17, 23, III 76n.

molde, *f.n-stem,* [MOULD¹]; soil I 195; ground II 210.

monaδ, *m.a-stem,* MONTH¹ III 120, 124, 224.

morδ, *n.a-stem,* [MURTH]; sinful deed II 173.

mōt, mōste, -on, *pret.* I 157, 207, etc; *pret.pres.*(6), [MOTE¹]; may III 236, etc.

g e m u n a n, *pret.pres.*(4), [I-MUNE]; remember III 208.

munuc, *m.a-stem,* MONK II 1, III 70, etc.

munuclīc, *adj.* [MONKLY]; monastic I 45.

munuclīce, *adv.* [MONK *sb.* + -LY²]; as a monk I 66.

munuclīf, *n.a-stem,* [MONK *sb.* + LIFE]; monastery III 372n.

gemyndig, *adj.* [MINDY]; mindful II 19, 88, 179.

mynster, *n.a-stem,* MINSTER¹, monastery I 91n, III 70, etc.

mynsterlīc, *adj.* [MINSTER¹ + -LY¹]; collegiate, monastic I 71.

mynsterman(n), *m.athem.stem,* [MINSTER¹ + MAN¹]; one of the clergy of a *mynster,* monk I 149, 156.

gemyntan, *w.v.*(1b), [I-MUNTE]; *w.inf. of vb. of motion omitted,* intend (to go) I 176.

myrcels, *m.a-stem,* trophy I 136.

N

nā, *adv.* [NA¹]; NO¹; not II 179.

nabban, *w.v.*(3), [NABBE]; have not II 48, 115, etc.

nāht, *n.* [NAUGHT]; nothing III 46, 136.

nama, *m.n-stem,* NAME I 105, III 30, 320.

nān, *pron.* NONE II 173; *adj.* no I 24, 46, etc; *adv.* no III 211.

nāteshwōn, *adv.* [NA WHON *(s.v.* WHON²)]; not in the least III 41.

nāδer, *adj.* NEITHER II 18.

nǣfre, *adv.* NEVER II 67, III 131, etc.

nægl, *m.a-stem,* NAIL II 160.

nǣs, *pret.ind. 3 sg.* II 67, etc; **nǣre,** *subj. 3 sg.* III 67; **nǣron,** *pret. 3 pl.* III 5, 120; *v.*(5), [NAS, NERE]; was not, were not.

ne, *adv.* [NE]; not I 24, 56, etc; *conj.* nor II 18, 70, etc; *ne . . . ne,* neither . . . nor III 235.

geneālēcan, *w.v.*(1b), [NEH-LECHE]; approach I 130, 131n.

nellan; nelle, *pres. 1 sg.* II 69, etc; **nele,** *pres. 3 sg.* III 36, etc; **nellaδ,** *pres.ind. pl.* II 205, etc; **nellon,** *pres.subj.pl.* III 365n; **nolde, -on,** *pret.* I 149, II 17, etc; *anom.v.* [NILL]; refuse, will not; *w.inf. of vb. of motion omitted,* III 40.

nexta, *sup.adj.* NEXT; *æt nextan,* next, finally III 52, etc.

nigon, *num.* NINE III 130, etc.

nigoða, *adj. NINTH* I 123.

niht, *f.athem.stem,* NIGHT I 31, 154, II 124, etc.

(ge)niman, *v.(4),* [NIM]; take I 81, 111, etc.

nis, *pres.ind. 3 sg.* [NIS]; is not I 225, II 214.

nīwan, *adv.* [NEWEN]; newly, recently III 317, 318.

nīwe, *adj.* NEW III 20.

nū, *adv.* NOW I 210, 211, etc; *conj.* now that I 225; since III 315; *correl. conj. and adv.* I 205–6*n.

nytan; nāt, *pres. I sg.* III 26; **nyste, -on,** *pret.* III 88, 172, etc; *pret.pres.(1),* [NOT¹]; know not.

nȳten, *n.a-stem,* [NETEN]; animal I 26.

O

of, *prep.w.dat.* OF I 47, 143, etc; out of III 349, etc; from I 97, III 105, 337, etc; *þe . . . of,* from whom III 179; *adv.* OFF II 106, etc; thereof, of it, I 217.

ofer, *prep.w.acc.* OVER I 151, II 1, etc; throughout I 154, etc.

ofersǣwisc, *adj. OVERSEA;* foreign; *as sb.* foreigner III 334.

oferwinnan, *v.(3),* [OVERWIN]; overcome I 34.

oferwȳrcan, *w.v.(1c),* [OVERWORK]; cover (with a gravestone) III 16.

ofhrēowan, *v.(2), w.gen.* [ARUE]; take pity on I 215n.

oflīcian, *w.v.(2), w.dat.* be displeasing to III 200.

ofslēan, *v.(6),* [OFSLAY]; slay II 30, 37*, 59, etc.

oft, *adv.* OFT, often I 235, II 125, etc.

ofwundrod, *adj.(p.pt.), w.gen.* amazed at II 133.

ōlǣcan, *w.v.(1b),* *w.dat.* [OLUHNEN]; fawn upon, be compliant towards III 300.

on, *prep.w.dat. or acc.* ON I 27, 66, etc; in I 2, 3, etc; into I 216, etc; with, by I 165, etc; *postponed,* against I 125; *þe . . . on,* on which I 192, etc.

onbryrdnys(s), *f.jō-stem,* fervour, I 97.

onbūtan, *prep.w.acc.* ABOUT, round III 351.

ondrǣdan, *v.(7), w.acc. and reflex.dat.* [ADREAD¹]; fear III 257.

ongēan, *adv. AGAIN;* back II 137.

onginnan, *v.(3),* [ONGIN]; begin I 37, III 144.

onlīhtan, *w.v.(1b),* [ONLIGHT¹]; restore to sight III 228.

onscunian, *w.v.(2),* [ASHUN]; detest III 69.

onuppon, *prep.w.dat.* [ANUPPE]; over, above; *postponed,* II 140.

geopenian, *w.v.(2),* OPEN III 32, 44.

orhlīce, *adv.* [ORGEL + LY²]; arrogantly, insolently II 194n.

orwēne, *adj.w.gen.* despairing of III 94, 250.

oð, *prep.w.acc.* until I 86, III 88, etc; as far as, to III 360; **oð þæt,** *conj.* until I 10, 29, etc.

ōðer, *adj. and pron.* OTHER I 61*, II 123, 202, etc; another III 286; the next I 20; one (of two) III 269; *se oðer . . . se oðer,* the one . . . the other III 232 f; *fram ende oð operne,* from one end to the other III 360 f.

oðöe, *conj.* [*OTHER*]; or I 48, 64, etc.

P

pāpa, *m.n-stem*, POPE[1] I 103, II 198.

paralisyn, *Latin acc.sg.* PARALYSIS I 177, III 149.

plega, *m.n-stem*, PLAY; sport III 243; playing of games III 256.

plegan, *v.*(5), plegian, *w.v.*(2), PLAY III 255n.

plegol, *adj.* given to playing games III 242.

post, *m.a-stem*, POST[1] I 187, etc.

prēost, *m.a-stem*, PRIEST, clerk I 199, III 22n, etc.

R

rād, *f.ō-stem*, [ROAD]; journey I 178.

rǣd, *adj.* RED II 150n.

rǣd, *m.a-stem*, [REDE[1]]; advice I 103; *him rǣd þuhte*, he thought it best II 53.

rǣdan, *w.v.*(1b), READ III 338.

rǣding, *f.ō-stem*, READING I 62; passage of scripture I 64.

rēafere, *m.ja-stem*, [REAVER] REIVER, robber III 299.

reccan, *w.v.*(1c), *w.gen.* RECK; care about II 40.

(ge)reccan, *w.v.*(1c), [RECCHE]; relate I 27, etc; explain, translate I 53.

gereccednys(s), *f.jō-stem*, account II 8.

gerēfa, *m.n-stem*, REEVE[1] II *126*.

reliquias, *m.pl.* relics I 212.

gereord, *n.a-stem*, [RERD(E)]; language I 54, 57.

rēðe, *adj.* [RETHE]; cruel, savage I 18, etc; harsh II 188, etc.

rīcceter(e), *n.* (act of) tyranny II 194.

rīce, *n.ja-stem*, [RICHE]; kingdom I 38, 71, etc.

rīce, *adj.* RICH I 48; mighty II 192.

rīdan, *v.*(1), RIDE I 65, 137, etc.

ridda, *m.n-stem*, rider, horseman I 176, 183.

(ge)rihtan, *w.v.*(1b), RIGHT; restore to health III 207.

gerihtlǣcan, *w.v.*(1b), [RIGHTLECHE]; direct I 114; amend III 42; correct III 77.

rihtlīce, *adv.* RIGHTLY, justly I 18.

rihtwīsnys(s), *f.jō-stem*, RIGHTEOUSNESS II 23.

rīxian, *w.v.*(2), reign I *236*, III 388.

rōd, *f.ō-stem*, ROOD, cross I 14, 16, etc.

rōf, *m.a-stem*, ROOF I 189n.

rōwan, *v.*(7), ROW[1]; sail II 33.

(ge)rȳman, *w.v.*(1b), [RIME[4]]; enlarge I 87.

S

sāgol, *m.a-stem*, [SOWEL]; cudgel II 92.

sagu, *f.ō-stem*, SAW[2]; story III 41.

samod, *adv.* also I 5; *mid . . . samod*, together with I 188.

sanct, *m.a-stem*, SAINT I 144n, 150, etc.

sancte, *fem.* SAINT II *216*n.

sand, *f.ō-stem*, [SAND[1]]; food I 79*n.

sand, *n.a-stem*, SAND[2] III 58.

sang, *m.a-stem*, SONG; singing (of hymns) III 116, 189, etc.

sārig, *adj.* SORRY; sorrowful II 115.

sārlīc, *adj.* [SORELY]; sorrowful I 205.

sāwl, *f.ō-stem*, SOUL I 133, 134, etc.

sāwllĕas, *adj.* SOULLESS; dead III 248.

sǣ, *f.i-stem,* SEA I 4, 145, etc.

sǣl, *m.i-stem,* [SELE]; occasion I 73, II 165.

gesǣlig, *adj.* [I-SELI]; blessed I 43, 115, etc; prosperous III 370.

gesǣliglīce, *adv.* [SEELILY]; happily II 23.

gesǣlð, *f.ō-stem,* [I-SELTH]; blessedness III 17.

scamel, *m.a-stem* [SHAMBLE¹]; stool III 360.

scafan, *v.(6),* SHAVE; shred I 216.

gescēadwīsnys(s), *f.jō-stem,* discretion, good sense I 67.

gesceaft, *f.i-stem,* [SHAFT¹]; creature III 54.

sceal(l), *pres.ind. 1 sg.* [205, *3 sg.* I 220, etc; **scealt,** *2 sg.* III 297; **sceolon,** *pl.* II 185, etc; **sc(e)olde,** *pret.sg.* II 40, 191, etc; **sceoldon,** *pret.pl.* I 64, etc; *pret.pres.(4),* SHALL, should, must, ought.

sceamel, see **scamel.**

sceamu, *f.ō-stem,* SHAME; *to sceame tucode,* shamefully ill-treated I 9.

sceanca, *m.n-stem,* SHANK; leg III 269.

scēawere, *m.ja-stem,* [SHOWER²]; spy, (hidden) spectator II 116.

scēawian, *w.v.(2),* [SHOW]; examine, scrutinize II 186, etc.

scēawung, *f.ō-stem,* [SHOWING]; looking, inspection II 202.

sceortlīce, *adv.* SHORTLY; briefly III 369.

scēotan, *v.(2),* SHOOT II 98.

scīnan, *v.(1),* SHINE III 284, etc.

scip, *n.a-stem,* SHIP¹ II 31, 110.

sciphere, *m.ja-stem,* [SHIP¹ + HERE]; naval force II 26n, 84, III 374.

scīr, *f.ō-stem,* SHIRE, district I 155.

scō(h), *m.a-stem,* SHOE III 105, 107.

scotung, *f.ō-stem,* SHOOTING II 152; missile II 100.

scrīn, *n.a-stem,* SHRINE I 143, etc.

Scyppend, *m.nd-stem,* [SHEP-PEND]; Creator I 201, III 54, 387.

scyttel, *m.a-stem,* [SHUTTLE²]; bolt III 349.

se, *nom.sg.m.* I 3, etc; **þone,** *acc.sg.m.* I 16, etc; **þæs,** *gen.sg.m.* I 30, etc, *neut.* I 42, etc; **þām,** *dat.sg.m.* I 39, etc, *neut.* I 6, etc, *dat.pl.* I 78, etc; **sēo,** *nom.sg.f.* I 24, etc; **þā,** *acc.sg.f.* I 27, etc, *nom.pl.* I 33, etc, *acc.pl.* I 9, etc; **þǣre,** *gen.sg.f.* I 145, etc, *dat.sg.f.* I 16, etc, *gen.pl.* III 7n; **þæt,** *nom.sg.n.* I 161, etc, *acc.sg.n.* I 48, etc; *dem.adj. and def.art.* THAT, THE I 9, 15, 91, etc; *dem.pron.* he III 56; to him III 304; they III 126, 264; those III 342; of those III 7; that I 42, 48, etc, *anticipating following clause,* II 63, 175, etc; *þæs on mergen,* next morning I 156, III 140; *rel. pron.* who I 3, 44, II 159, etc; to whom III 80; as III 385; that which I 221; **se þe,** who II 34, 208, etc; he who III 216, 317; **þone þe,** whom I 157 f, III 324; **þā þe,** who I 165, III 255; those who(m) II 181, III 309; **þām þe,** to, for those who II 125, 184; **þæt þæt,** that which III 246 f; see also **þām, þan, þæs, þē.**

sealm, *m.a-stem,* PSALM I 64.

sēcan, *w.v.(1c),* SEEK, search (for) II 120, 124, III 107.

gesēcan, *w.v.*(*1c*), [I-SECHE]; reach III 126; visit, go to I 195, III 84, etc.

secgan, *w.v.*(*3*), *SAY*[1], tell II 109, III 30, etc.

seldon, *adv. SELDOM* I 65.

sēlost, *sup.adv.* [SELE + -EST]; best II 139n, III 301.

sēlra, *comp.adj.* [SELE + -ER[3]]; better III 97n.

sendan, *w.v.*(*1*), SEND[1] I 39, 41, etc.

sēo, see **se.**

sēoc, *adj.* SICK III 296.

seofon, *num.* SEVEN II 202, III 121, etc.

seolcen, *adj.* SILKEN II 150.

seolfor, *n.a-stem,* SILVER I 143, II 163.

gesēon, *v.*(*5*), [I-SEE]; SEE I 131, III 175, 209, etc; look on III 175; *in pass.* appear, be thought III 49.

gesetnys(s), *f.jō-stem,* [I-SETNESSE]; treatise II 199; foundation I 72n.

(ge)settan, *w.v.*(*1c*), [I-SET]; SET, put III 59, 346; set up I 136; set down II 8, etc; appoint II 188, III 137, etc; *settan to,* appoint as II 12, 20.

sibb, *f.jō-stem,* [SIB[1]]; peace II 142, III 373.

gesib(b), *adj.* [I-SIB]; related III 72.

gesicclian, *w.v.*(*2*), [SICKLE]; to be taken ill I 170.

sige, *m.i-stem,* [SIYE]; victory I 21, II 32.

sigefæst, *adj.* [SIYE + FAST]; victorious II 43.

gesihð, *f.ō-stem,* [I-SIGHT]; SIGHT[1] III 168, 356, etc; vision III 48, 322.

singal, *adj.* continual I 93.

singan, *v.*(*3*), SING[1] III 136, etc.

sittan, *v.*(*5*), SIT I 73, 77, etc.

sīð, *m.a-stem,* [SITHE[1]]; time III 50, 194.

sīðian, *w.v.*(*2*), [SITHE[1]]; journey I 5, 66, 115, etc.

sīððan, *adv.* [SITHEN]; afterwards I 20, 24, 35, etc; *conj.* SINCE III 165; after II 112.

slāpan, *v.*(*7*), *SLEEP* III 194.

slǣp, *m.a-stem,* SLEEP I 31, III 210, 322; *weard on slæpe,* fell asleep I 179 f, III 102 f.

slǣwð, *f.ō-stem,* [SLEUTH[1]]; SLOTH[1] III 201.

slēan, *v.*(*6*), *SLAY*[1] I 9, II 26; strike II 168; cut II 106; pitch (a tent) I 150.

slecg, *f.jō-stem,* SLEDGE[1]; hammer II 168.

slege, *m.i-stem,* [SLAY[1]]; slaying I 13, II 106n, etc.

smēagan, *w.v.*(*2*), think I 37, etc; consider II 50, etc.

smið, *m.a-stem,* SMITH; craftsman (in metal, wood, stone, etc) III 21, 25, etc.

snotor, *adj.* [SNOTER]; wise II 14.

sōna, *adv.* SOON I 4, 43, etc; immediately I 75, 215, etc; **sona swa, sona . . . swa,** *conj.* as soon as I 38, 174, etc.

sōð, *adj.* [SOOTH]; true I 67, 106, II 24n, etc; *to soðan,* III 31, etc, *to soðum,* III 244 truly.

sōðlīce, *adv.* [SOOTHLY]; truly III 238, 337.

spadu, *f.ō-stem,* SPADE[1] II 170.

spearca, *m.n-stem,* SPARK[1] I 189.

spēd, *f.i-stem,* [SPEED]; wealth; *plur.w.sg.meaning,* III 302.

sprǣc, *f.jō-stem,* SPEECH[1] I 56, II 204; *æt spræce,* in conversation II 4 f.

sprecan, *v.*(*5*), SPEAK III 56, 252; tell III 113.

GLOSSARY

gesprecan, *v.*(5), speak with III
50.

staca, *m.n-stem*, STAKE[1] I 138.

stalu, *f.ō-stem*, [STALE[1]]; steal-
ing III 220.

stān, *m.a-stem*, STONE III 57.

standan, *v.*(6), STAND III 87,
293, etc; be fixed III 58, etc;
remain III 117n; shine forth I
153.

stæf, *m.a-stem*, STAFF[1] III 348n.

stǣnen, *adj.* [STONEN]; stone III
19.

stede, *m.i-stem*, [STEAD]; place I
196.

stelan, *v.*(4), STEAL[1] II 166.

stemn,*f.ō-stem*, [STEVEN[1]]; voice
I 205.

gestillan, *w.v.*(*1*), [I-STILL]; re-
strain, stop II 201.

stocc, *m.a-stem*, STOCK[1]; stake I
213.

stōw, *f.wō-stem*, [STOW[1]]; place
I 32, 175, etc.

strand, *n.a-stem*, STRAND[1], shore
I 145.

strǣt, *f.ō-stem or uninflected*,
STREET I 77.

gestrēon, *n.a-stem*, [I-STREON];
treasure II 46.

strūtian, *w.v.*(*2*), [STRUT[1]]; exert
oneself, strive (to force an
entry) II 172n.

stȳran, *w.v.*(*1*), *w.dat.* STEER[1];
restrain, reprove, punish II 23.

sum, *adj.* SOME, a certain, a(n) I
1, 27, 30, etc; one I 73, etc;
w.numerals, some III 282;
pron. one II 168 ff, 175 f;
some III 157 f, 338.

gesund, *adj.* [I-SOUND]; un-
corrupted II 195.

gesundful, *adj.* [I-SUNDFUL];
uncorrupted I 86.

sunnbēam, *m.a-stem*, SUNBEAM
I 154.

sunne, *f.n-stem*, SUN I 97, III
131.

sūpan, *v.*(*2*), SUP[1]; drink I 217.

sūð, *adv.* SOUTH, southwards I
198.

sūðan, *adv.* from the south II 1.

suwian, *w.v.*(*2*), [SWIE]; be
silent II 54.

swa, *adv.* SO, thus I 57, II 76,
etc; *swa . . . þæt*, *swa þæt*,
so . . . that, so that II 16 f,
III 45, etc; in as much as, in
that I 63, II 62, etc; that I
52 f, 125, etc; *swa . . . swilce*,
as . . . as if III 57 f; see also
eallswa, and **swa**, *conj.*

swa, *conj.* as I 141, II 172, etc;
sona swa, *sona . . . swa*, see
sona; *swa* (*adv.*) *. . . swa*
(*conj.*), as . . . as I 145, II 128,
etc; *swa hwær* (*hwæt*, *hwider*)
swa, see **hwær**, etc; **swa swa**,
conj. as, just as I 21, II 5, etc;
like II 21 f, etc; *swa* (*adv.*) *. . .
swa swa* (*conj.*), in the same
way . . . as I 61, III 236; see
also **swilc**.

swāra, see **swǣr(e)**.

swārlīce, *adv.* [SWEER *adj.* +
-LY[2]]; painfully III 217.

swaðēah, *adv.* however, never-
theless III 10, 53, etc.

swǣr(e), *adj.* [SWEER]; painful,
oppressive III 352.

swefn, *n.a-stem*, [SWEVEN];
dream III 21, 56n, etc.

sweltan, *v.*(3), [SWELT]; die I
132n, II 201, etc.

(ge)swencan, *w.v.*(*1b*),
[SWENCHE]; afflict II 142.

swencg, *m.i-stem*, [SWENG];
stroke II 106.

geswīcan, *v.*(*1*), [I-SWIKE];
cease II 142, 202, etc.

swicdōm, *m.a-stem*, [SWIKE-
DOM]; deception III 339.

swilc, *adj.* SUCH II 139, 221, etc; like (him) II 206; *swilce . . . swilce* (*conj.*), such . . . as II 215; *swilce . . . swa swa* (*conj.*), such . . . as III 378 f.

swilce, *conj.* [SUCH]; like I 153, II 100; as it were II 99, 150, etc; *w.subj.* as if II 136, III 104, etc; see also **eallswa, swa,** *adv.,* **swilc.**

swilce, *adv.* see **ēac.**

swincan, *v.*(*3*), [SWINK]; labour I 92, II 171.

swingan, *v.*(*3*), SWING[1]; scourge II 95.

swingel(l), *f.ō-stem,* SWINGLE; stroke (of whip) II 96, III 142; *to swinglum,* to be whipped III 138.

swipu, *f.ō-stem, or* **swipe,** *f.n-stem,* [SWEPE[1]]; whip II 95.

geswogen, *adj.*(*p.pt.*), [SWOW]; in a swoon III 248.

swura, *m.n-stem,* [SWIRE]; neck II 149, 150.

swurdbora, *m.n-stem,* SWORD-bearer II 6, 7.

swustor, *f.r-stem,* SISTER II 217.

swutel, *adj.* [SUTEL]; clear, manifest II 206, III 10.

geswutelian, *w.v.*(*2*), [SUTELE]; make clear, reveal III 3, 10, etc.

swutelung, *f.ō-stem,* evidence, indication II 151, III 357.

swȳðe, *adv.* [SWITH]; very I 35, 69, etc; much, greatly I 87, 193, etc; violently II 168; severely III 269; **swiðor,** *comp.* more I 93; rather II 68, III 257, etc; **swȳðost,** *sup.* most III 384.

swȳðlic, *adj.* [SWITH + -LY[1]]; great I 82, 97.

swȳðra, *comp.adj.* [SWITHER]; right I 82, etc; *as sb.* right hand I 84*n.

sȳferlice, *adv.* chastely II 160.

sylf, *adj.* SELF I 133, II 223, etc; himself I 18, 222, III 32n, etc; thyself III 303; ourselves III 218; themselves III 357.

sylfren, *adj.* [SILVERN]; silver I 75n, 79.

sylfwyll, *a-stem,* [SELFWILL]; *gen. as adv.* voluntarily I 221.

syllan, *w.v.*(*1c*), [SELL]; give I 80, 212, etc.

syllic, *adj.* [SELLY]; marvellous III 11.

sym(b)le, *adv.* unceasingly, always I 60, II 15, etc.

syndrig, *adj.* [SUNDRY]; private I 96.

gesȳne, *adj.* [SENE]; visible III 87.

synful(l), *adj.* SINFUL III 55, 77.

syx, *num.* SIX III 121.

syxtȳne, *num.* SIXTEEN III 122.

T

tācn, *n.a-stem,* TOKEN; sign, miracle III 11, 112, 362n.

tam, *adj.* TAME II 136.

tāwian, *w.v.*(*2*), [TAW[1]]; ill-treat II 56; see **bysmor.**

tǣlan, *w.v.*(*1b*), [TELE]; disparage III 298.

geteld, *n.a-stem,* [TELD]; tent I 151, 153.

getellan, *w.v.*(*1c*), [I-TELLE]; count III 124.

tēon, *v.*(*2*), [TEE[1]]; drag away II 105; lift III 57; instruct, teach I 62; *forð teon,* perpetrate III 256.

tēonful, *adj.* [TEENFUL]; hurtful, slanderous III 298.

tīd, *f.i-stem,* TIDE; time III 138.

tīgan, *w.v.*(*1b*), TIE II 94.

tige, *m.i-stem,* pull III 39, 40.

tīma, *m.n-stem*, TIME I 100, III 34, etc.

getīmian, *w.v.(2)*, *impers.w.dat.* [TIME]; befall I 178.

getīōian, *w.v.(2)*, *w.dat. of person and gen. or dat. of thing*, [TITHE¹]; grant I 41, 43n, etc.

to, *prep.w.dat.* TO I 1, 4, 13, 14n, etc; *w.infl.inf.* I 19, III 235n, etc; in addition to II 116; close to II 138; according to III 42; as, for I 88, 136, etc; for I 115; *postponed*, I 11, 83, etc; *þe . . . to*, to which I 52; *þær . . . to*, to the place to which I 185 f; *w.gen.* II 99n.

tō, *adv.* thereto I 138, II 113; at him II 99n; TOO III 336.

toberstan, *v.(3)*, [TOBURST]; break I 28, III 268, 353.

toceorfan, *v.(3)*, [TOCARVE]; cut in pieces I 80.

tocyme, *m.i-stem*, [TOCOME]; advent III 258.

togædere, *adv.* TOGETHER I 129, II 143; see **fōn**.

togēanes, *prep.w.dat.* [TOGAINS]; against, at; *postponed*, II 99.

tōl, *n.a-stem*, TOOL II 173.

tomiddes, *prep.w.dat.* [TOMIDS]; among I 188.

towerd, *adj.* [TOWARD]; future, (who were) to come after III 9.

trēow, *n.wa-stem*, TREE II 93; (piece of) wood, stake I 216.

getrymman, *w.v.(1a)*, [TRIM]; strengthen I 13.

trymming, *f.ō-stem*, strengthening II 217.

tūcian, *w.v.(2)*, [TUCK¹]; illtreat I 9, II 38; punish III 229.

tūn, *m.a-stem*, TOWN; village II 136.

twēgen, *nom.m.* I 8n, etc; **twā**, *nom.n.* III 123, etc; **twām**,

dat. III 73, etc; *num.* [TWAIN]; TWO.

twelf, *num.* TWELVE III 122, 124.

twentig, *num.* TWENTY II 34, III 156.

tȳn, *num.* TEN III 122.

þ

þā, *adv.* [THO]; then I 14, 19, etc; *þa . . . þa . . . þa*,   then . . . when . . . then II 141 f; **þā**, when I 124, 226, etc; *þa þa . . . þa*, when . . . then II 9, III 1–3; since . . . then III 290.

þā, see **se**.

þāgīt, *adv.* yet I 57; still I 102, 107, etc.

þam, þan, *dat. and instr. sg.n. dem.pron.*, *used to form adv. and (with the addition of þe) conj.* [THAN]; see **æfter, ær, betwux**, etc; see also **se**.

þancian, *w.v.(2)*, *w.dat. of pers. and gen. of thing*, THANK II 134, III 155, etc.

þanon, *adv.* [THENNE]; THENCE II 174, III 60, etc.

þās, see **þes**.

þær, *adv.* THERE I 4, 21, etc; where I 40, 138, etc; to, or from, the place where I 166, 173, etc; **þær þær**, where III 288.

þærbinnan, *adv.* [THERE + BIN]; therein I 113.

þære, see **se**.

þærrihte, *adv.* [THERERIGHT]; at once III 270.

þærtō, *adv.* THERETO, to it II 94.

þærtoēacan, *adv.* [THERE-TEKEN]; in addition to that, furthermore III 378.

þæs, *gen.sg.n.dem.pron. as adv.*
[THES]; therefore I 236, II 227,
III 277; **þæs ðe,** *conj.* as III
103; see also **se.**

þæt, see **se.**

þæt, *conj.* THAT I 16, 18, etc;
repeated, III 44; (namely) that
II 200, etc; *w.proleptic pron.
in main cl.* II 64, III 8, 114;
with the result that I 28, etc;
in order that I 51, etc; see also
swa.

þe, *indecl.rel.pron.* [THE]; who I
5, etc; whom II 72; which,
that I 25, 123, etc; in which II
33; see also **se, þam, þan,
þæs, þeah.**

þe, se **þu.**

þē, *adv. (instr.sg.n.dem.pron.)
w.comp.* THE I 222, III 277,
343.

þeah þe, *conj.* THOUGH II 209,
222, etc.

þearf, *f.ō-stem,* [THARF]; need I
201n; advantage I 50.

þearfa, *m.n-stem,* poor man I 48,
77, etc.

þearflīc, *adj.* necessary III 67.

þearle, *adv.* grievously III 79;
abundantly II 163.

þeaw, *m.wa-stem,* [THEW¹]; *in
pl.* manner of life, conduct I 70,
208, etc.

þegn, þēnas, *nom.pl.* II 186;
m.a-stem, THANE¹, retainer I
76, II 65, III 149, etc;
servant II 186.

þegnian, *w.v.(2), w.dat.*[THEINE];
serve II 184.

þencan, *w.v.(1c),* THINK III 303.

þēnung, *f.ō-stem,* THEINING; *in
pl.* banquet I 75.

þēod, *f.ō-stem,* [THEDE]; nation
I 88.

þēof, *m.a-stem,* THIEF II 165, III
300, etc.

þēon, *v.(1) or (2), (orig. (3)),*
[THEE¹]; thrive III 2.

þēos, see **þes.**

þēow, *adj.* [THEOW]; bond III
345.

þēow, *m.wa-stem,* **þēowa,**
m.n-stem, [THEOW]; slave III
350; servant II 212, III 13.

þēowdōm, *m.a-stem,* [THEOW-
DOM]; service II 212.

þes, *nom.sg.m.* I 84*, II 215n,
etc; **þisne, þysne,** *acc.sg.m.* I
18, II 154; **þysum,** *dat.sg.m.*
II 206, III 276, *neut.* II 80,
III 55, etc, *dat.pl.* II 66, 72,
III 112; **þēos,** *nom.sg.f.* I 84;
þās, *acc.sg.f.* I 224, II 227, etc,
nom.pl. II 56, 60, *acc.pl.* I 220,
II 180, III 22; **þysre,** *gen.
sg.f.* III 367, *dat.sg.f.* III 6;
þis, *nom.sg.n.* II 198, *acc.sg.n.*
I 86, II 108, etc; *dem.adj. and
pron.* THIS, THESE; *oð þis,* to
this day I 86.

þicce, *adj.* THICK, dense II
111.

þicgan, *v.(5),* [THIG]; take,
drink I 168.

þīn, *adj.* THINE; THY II 45, 46n,
etc.

þincan, *w.v.(1c), impers.w.dat.*
THINK¹; seem III 103, 104, etc;
wæs him geðuht, he thought II
118.

þin(c)g, *n.a-stem,* THING¹ I 46,
70, etc.

geþincð, *f.ō-stem,* high position;
pl.w.sg.meaning, I 95, III 77.

þingian, *w.v.(2), w.dat. of person
for whom and prep. to w.dat.
of person with whom,* [THING];
intercede I 210, III 181, 238n.

þingung, *f.ō-stem,* intercession
III 160, 230.

þis, þisne, see **þes.**

þone, see **se.**

GLOSSARY

þonne, *adv.* THEN III 39, 40, etc; when I 222, II 214, etc.

þonne, *conj.* THAN I 93, II 213.

þrǣd, *m.a-stem*, THREAD II 150.

þrēagan, *w.v.(2)*, [THREA]; rebuke III 50.

þrēo, see þrȳ.

þrittig, *num.* THIRTY I 124.

þriwa, *adv.* [THRIE]; THRICE III 57, 193.

þrūh, *f.athem.stem*, [THROUGH¹]; coffin III 19, 38.

þrȳ, *nom.m.* III 121, *acc.m.* II 190; þrēo, *nom.n.* III 129; þrym, III 18, etc, þrim, II 3, *dat.*; *num.* THREE.

þrydda, *adj.* THIRD III 50, 130.

þrymwealdende, *adj.* [THRUM *sb.*¹ + WIELDING]; who rules glory III 239n.

þu, *nom.* I 211, 214, etc; þe, *acc.* I 212, etc, *dat.* III 182, etc; *pron.* THOU, THEE; *reflex.dat.* II 62.

geþungen, *adj.(orig. p.pt. of þēon)*, perfect (in virtue), faultless II 16.

þurfan; þorfte, *pret. 1 sg.* II 68; *pret.pres.(3)*, [THARF]; must.

þurh, *prep.w.acc.* THROUGH II 129, 179, 220, III 40, etc; by II 28, 76, III 24, 86, etc; by the grace of III 2, etc.

þurhwunian, *w.v.(2)*,[THROUGH- + WON]; continue II 17.

þus, *adv.* THUS I 83, 133.

(ge)þwǣrlǣcan, *w.v.(1b)*, *w.dat. or prep.* give assent, be a party to II 185, III 300; conspire, associate with III 299.

þwēan, *v.(6)*, wash I 158.

þyder, *adv.* THITHER II 167; whither I 176n.

þȳfel, *m.a-stem*, [THYVEL]; bush II 120.

þyllīc, *adj.* [THELLIC]; such III 362.

þȳn, *w.v.(1b)*, press III 59.

þȳrl, *n.a-stem*, [THIRL¹]; hole III 59.

þyrstan, *w.v.(1b),impers.w.dat.* THIRST III 313.

þysne, þysre, þysum, see þes.

U

uhtsang, *m.a-stem*, [UHTSONG]; Nocturns, Lauds I 95n.

under, *prep.w.dat.* UNDER III 2.

underdelfan, *v.(3)*, [UNDERDELVE]; dig under II 169.

underfōn, *v.(7)*, [UNDERFO]; receive I 50, 88, 150, etc.

underkyning, *m.a-stem*, UNDERKING II 47.

undōn, *anom.v.* UNDO; open III 93.

unēaðe, *adv.* [UNEATH]; hardly III 93.

unforht, *adj.* unafraid II 73.

unformolsnod, *adj.(p.pt.)*, uncorrupted II 156.

ungefullod, *adj.(p.pt.)*, [UN-¹ + YFULLED]; unbaptized I 128.

ungemetlīce, *adv.* [UN-¹ + I-MET + LY²]; excessively III 242.

ungesǣlig, *adj.* [UN-¹ + I-SELI]; wretched, wicked II 165, 188.

unhāl, *adj.* [UNWHOLE]; sick III 128, 356.

unlūcan, *v.(2)*, [UNLOUK]; open II 170.

unnan; ūðe, *pret. 3 sg.* I 22; *pret.pres.(3)*, [UNNE]; grant.

unrihtlīce, *adv.* [UNRIGHTLY]; wickedly III 260.

unscyldig, *adj.* [UN-¹ + SHILDY]; innocent III 221.

unseldon, *adv.* [UNSELDE]; often III 219.

113

unsōŏsagul, *adj.* untruthful III 49.

untrum, *adj.* [UNTRUM]; infirm, sick I 26, III 110, 281; *as sb.* III 101, 121.

untrumnys(s), *f.jō-stem,* [UNTRUMNESS]; infirmity I 225.

geuntrumod, *adj.(p.pt.),* afflicted III 156*n; *w.dat. or prep.* afflicted with III 92, 264; *wearŏ geuntrumod,* fell ill I 202 f.

unŏēaw, *m.wa-stem,* [UNTHEW]; *in pl.* evil ways III 24.

unwīslīce, *adv.* UNWISELY; foolishly III 254.

unwittig, *adj.* [UNWITTY]; foolish II 193; innocent II 37.

upgang, *m.a-stem,* rising I 97.

up(p), *adv.* UP[1] I 98, 159, etc.

uppon, *prep.w.dat.* [UP[1]]; upon, on II 175*n.

ūre, *adj.* OUR I 19, 134, II 42.

ūs, see we.

ūt, *adv.* OUT II 181, III 222, etc.

ūtdrǣf, *m.f. or n.i-stem,* expulsion III 71n.

uton, *auxiliary v., forming w. inf. imp. 1 pers. pl.* [UTE]; *uton feallan,* let us fall I 16.

W

wacian, *w.v.(2),* WAKE; keep watch III 99, 102, etc.

wāg, *m.a-stem,* [WOUGH[1]]; wall III 361.

wanhafol, *adj.* poor III 301.

wan(n)hāl, *adj.* [WAN- + WHOLE]; sick III 119, etc; *as sb.* I 168, 227.

waru, *f.ō-stem,* [WARE[2]]; defence I 123.

wǣdla, *m.n-stem,* [WÆDLE[2]]; person in want I 48, II 21.

wǣlegode, see weligian.

wælhrēow, *adj.* cruel I 34, II 82.

wælhrēowlīce, *adv.* horribly II 196.

wælhrēownys(s), *f.jō-stem,* savagery II 32.

wǣpn, *n.a-stem,* WEAPON II 88n, 90.

wæs, *pret.ind. 1, 3 sg.* I 1, III 317, etc; wǣre, *subj. 2 sg.* II 74n, *3 sg.* I 199, etc; wǣron, *pret.pl.* I 52, etc; *v.(5),* WAS, WERE; *w.p.pt. of vbs. of motion forming pluperf.* I 52, 110, etc.

wæter, *n.a-stem,* WATER I 161, 163, etc.

we, *nom.* I 18, 141, etc; ūs, *acc.* I 17, etc, *dat.* I 27, etc; *pron.* WE, US; *reflex.* III 236.

gewealdan, *v.(7),* *w.gen.* WIELD; rule I 38, 123.

Wealdend, *m.nd-stem,* [WALDEND]; Lord I 21.

wealhstod, *m.a-stem,* interpreter I 55.

weall, *m.a-stem,* WALL[1] I 33.

wealwian, *w.v.(2),* WALLOW[1]; roll I 170, 172n.

weard, see wiŏ.

wearg, *m.a-stem,* [WARY]; criminal II 175.

gewēd, *n.i-stem,* madness, foolish behaviour III 258.

weg, *m.a-stem,* WAY[1] I 176; *be wæge,* on the way II 81–2n.

wegfarende, *adj.* WAYFARING; on a journey I 169n.

wel, *adv.* WELL I 55, III 305, etc.

weldǣd, *f.i-stem,* [WELDEDE]; benefit III 364.

welig,*adj.*[WEALY[1]]; rich III 161.

weligian; wǣlegode, *pret.subj. 3 sg.* II 211; *w.v.(2),* [AWELGIEN]; make rich.

welwillende, *adj.* [WELL-WILLING]; benevolent I 49, III 387.

GLOSSARY

welwillendnys(s), *f.jō-stem*, [*WELL-WILLINGNESS*]; benevolence II 22.

geweman, *w.v.(1b)*, win over I 42.

wēnan, *w.v.(1b)*, [WEEN]; think I 23, III 89, 270.

(ge)wendan, *w.v.(1b)*, [1-WENDE]; WEND; turn I 218, etc; go II 11, 81, etc; *w.reflex.dat.* III 160.

wēofod, *n.a-stem*, [WEVED]; altar II 161, III 295.

weorc, *n.a-stem*, WORK, task II 176; deed I 60, 202, etc; execution III 51.

geweorc, *n.a-stem*, building III 20.

wer, *m.a-stem*, [WERE¹]; man I 199, II 37n, III 92, etc; husband III 325; *se halga wer*, the saint I 169, 194, etc.

werod, *n.a-stem*, [WERED]; force(s), army I 12, 23, etc.

wīde, *adv.* far and WIDE I 197, II 26, etc.

wīdgil(l), *adj.* extensive I 172.

wīf, *n.a-stem*, WIFE II 66, etc; woman II 37, etc.

willa, *m.n-stem*, WILL¹ I 37, etc.

willan; wille, *pres. 1 sg.* II 76, etc, *3 sg.subj.* III 182; wile, *3 sg.ind.* I 17; wylt, *2 sg.* I 214, etc; willað, *3 pl.* III 206; wolde, *pret.sg.* I 38, etc; woldon, *pret.pl.* II 145, etc; *anom.v.* WILL, would I 104, III 182, etc; wish I 38, II 47, etc; be willing I 206, 214, etc; use (to) I 95, 226, etc; be about (to) III 102, 295.

(ge)wilnian, *w.v.(2)*, *w.gen.* [WILNE]; desire I 46, II 64.

windan, *v.(3)*, WIND¹; fly I 189.

gewinn, *n.ja-stem*, [1-WIN]; battle I 15.

winnan, *v.(3)*, [WIN¹]; fight I 18, 125, II 90.

gewinnan, *v.(3)*, [1-WIN]; win I 21, II 32.

wintersetl, *n.a-stem*, [WINTER¹ + SETTLE¹]; winter quarters II 45.

(ge)wiscan, *w.v.(1b)*, *w.gen.* WISH II 64, 223.

gewislīce, *adv.* [IWISLICHE]; clearly III 63, 81.

gewis(s), *adj.* [(I)WIS]; *to gewissan*, for certain III 27.

gewissian, *w.v.(2)*, [1-WISSE]; direct II 22.

gewissost, *sup.adv.* most certainly III 91.

wissung, *f.ō-stem*, [WISSING]; guidance II 123; rule III 377.

wita, *m.n-stem*, [WITE¹]; counsellor I 53n.

witan, III 244, etc; wāt, *pres. 1 sg.* I 209, *3 sg.* I 18, etc; wāst, *2 sg.* III 320; wiste, *pret. 3 sg.* III 91, 305; *pret. pres.(1)*, [WIT¹]; know; *is to witenne*, it should be understood III 235n, etc.

gewītan, *v.(1)*, [1-WITE²]; depart III 75.

wītega, *m.n-stem*, [WITIE]; prophet II 180.

witodlīce, *adv.* verily, indeed, in fact I 103, II 73, III 28.

wið, *prep.w.acc.* WITH II 46, 50; in comparison with III 46; against I 18, etc; from I 17, etc; by I 33, etc; *wið* ... *weard*, [WITH ... -WARD(4)]; towards I 99n; *w.gen.* towards I 189; *w.dat.(instr.)*, wið þam þe, *conj.* provided that II 57.

wiðersæc, *n.a-stem*, [WITHER-¹ + SAKE]; apostasy I 52n.

wiðfeohtan, *v.(3)*, *w.dat.* [WITH- + FIGHT]; fight against I 12.

115

wiðinnan, *prep.w.dat.* WITHIN III 19.

wiðsacan, *v.(6)*, *w.acc. or dat.* deny, reject II 102, 222n.

wiðstandan, *v.(6)*, *w.dat.* WITHSTAND I 24, II 48.

wōd, *adj.* [WOOD]; *as sb.* lunatic I 171.

wōdlīce, *adv.* [WOODLY]; insanely II 97.

wōdnys(s), *f.jō-stem*, [WOODNESS]; madness I 165n.

woffian, *w.v.(2)*, rave, blaspheme III 247.

wōhnys(s), *f.jō-stem*, [WOUGH *adj.* + -NESS]; perversity, wickedness I *165*.

wōlīce, *adv.* [WOUGH *adj.* + -LY²]; wrongly, unjustly III 229.

wōp, *m.a-stem*, [WOP]; weeping III 141.

word, *n.a-stem*, WORD II 72, 180, III 22, etc.

woruld, *f.ō-stem*, (this) WORLD, earth I 94, 232, etc; (the next) world I 228; mankind, men II 193, etc; *a to worulde*, for ever and ever I 236.

woruldcaru, *f.ō-stem*, [WORLD + CARE¹]; worldly care I 45.

worulddōm, *m.a-stem*, [WORLD + DOOM]; sentence of a civil court III 222.

gewrit, *n.a-stem*, [I-WRIT]; writing II 205.

wucu, *f.n-stem*, WEEK III 265.

wudewe, see wydewe.

wudu, *m.u-stem*, WOOD¹ II 120, etc.

wuldor, *n.a-stem*, [WULDER]; glory I 232, 236, etc.

wulf, *m.a-stem*, WOLF II 36, etc.

gewuna, *m.n-stem*, [I-WUNE]; custom; *on gewunon*, regularly III 218n.

wund, *f.ō-stem*, WOUND II 151.

wundor, *n.a-stem*, WONDER, miracle I 220n, 225, III 4, etc.

wundorlīce, *adv.* [WONDERLY]; wondrously, miraculously II 172, III 198, etc.

wundrian, *w.v.(2)*, WONDER, marvel I 155; *w.gen.* marvel at I 193n, etc.

gewunelīc, *adj.* [I-WUNE + -LY¹]; customary II 67, etc.

wunian, *w.v.(2)*, [WON]; remain, continue III 224, etc; endure I 36; dwell III 27, etc.

wurð, *adj.* WORTH III 46.

wurðan, *v.(3)*, [WORTH¹]; become, be I 147, 214*n, etc; *freq.w.p.pt.* forming *pass.* I 4, 6, etc; occur II 144, etc; *wearð to*, became, proved I 164.

gewurðan, *v.(3)*, [I-WORTH]; come III 341; *gewearð be*, happen to, befall I 125.

wurðful(l), *adj.* [WORTHFUL]; estimable, venerable II 15, 210, etc.

wurðian, *w.v.(2)*, [WORTH²]; venerate I 119, etc; glorify I 91, etc.

wurðlīce, *adv.* [WORTHLY]; splendidly, reverently II 143, III 21, 116.

wurðmynt, *m.* (*orig. f. ō-stem*), [WORTHMINT]; honour, glory I 14, etc; veneration I 25, etc.

wydewe, wudewe, *f.n-stem*, WIDOW¹ II 21, 157.

(ge)wyldan, *w.v.(1b)*, [I-WELDE]; WIELD; subdue II 44.

wȳln, *f.ō-stem*, serving woman III 138.

wynsum, *adj.* WINSOME; delightful III 210, 341*, 370.

GLOSSARY

(ᵹe)wyrcan, *w.v.(1c)*, [I-WURCHE]; *WORK*; perform II 227, etc; make I 188; build I 34n, etc; *w.gen., worhte fleames*, took to flight II 67.

wyri(ᵹ)an, *w.v.(1b)*, [WARY]; curse III 298, 309, 309*.

ᵹewyrpan, *w.v.(1b)*, recover I 217.

wyrðe, *adj.* [WURTHE]; worthy; *wyrðe beon, w.gen. or clause,* deserve I 209, II 74, 210.

Y

yfel, *adj.* EVIL II 201; painful I1 197, III 92.

yfel, *n.a-stem,* EVIL, ill III 297, etc.

yfeldǣd, *f.i-stem,* [EVIL + DEED]; evil deed III 300.

yfelnys(s), *f.jō-stem,* [EVIL-NESS]; wickedness I 11.

ylca, *adj.* [ILK¹]; same I 24, 27, 31, etc.

yld, *f.ō-stem,* [ELD²]; age I 124*.

yldra, *m.n-stem,* *(comp.adj.),* ELDER; ancestor II 46.

yrmð, *f.ō-stem,* [ERMTH(E)]; misery III 175.

yrnan, *v.(3),* RUN III 145, 284, etc; *w.reflex.dat.pron.* III 172.

yrre, *adj.* [IRRE]; angry II 98; *w.dat.* angry with III 345.

GLOSSARY OF PROPER NAMES

Abbo, *nom.* Abbo II 4, 11.

Aidan, *nom.* I 44, etc; **Aidanus,** *nom.* I 81, etc, **Aidanes,** *gen.* I 231; (St) Aidan.

Angle, *m.i-stem pl.* [ANGLE²]; the English I 89.

Angelcynn, *n.ja-stem,* [ANGLE³ + KIN¹]; the English nation, England II 214, etc.

Angol, *nom.* England II *214.*

Antecrist, *m.a-stem,* Antichrist III 366.

Augustinus, *nom.* (St) Augustine I 1n.

Aðelwold, *m.a-stem,* (St) Athelwold III 14n, 24, etc.

Ælfred, *m.a-stem,* (King) Alfred II 33n.

Æðeldryð, *f.i-stem,* (St) Æthelthryth (Audrey) II 216n.

Æðelred, *m.a-stem,* (King) Æthelred II 2.

Æðelstan, *m.a-stem,* (King) Athelstan II 6.

Bardanig, *f.jō-stem,* Bardney (Lincs.) I 148n.

Bebbanburh, *f.athem.stem,* Bamburgh (Northumberland) I 144n.

Beda, *nom.* Bede I 27, 224.

Benedictes, *gen.* (St) Benedict II 2n.

Birinus, *nom.* I 101, etc; **Birine,** *dat.* I 112; (St) Birinus.

Bryt(t), *m.a-stem,* [BRIT]; Briton I 7, 89.

Ce(a)dwalla, *m.n-stem,* Cedwalla I 7n, 9, 23, 127.

Ceaster, *f.ō-stem,* [CHESTER¹]; Winchester (Hants.) III 332n.

Crist, *m.a-stem,* CHRIST I 7, etc.

Cumera, *gen.pl.* the Cumbrians, the Britons of Strathclyde III 375.

Cūðberht, *m.a-stem,* (St) Cuthbert I 230, II 216n.

Cwichel, *m.a-stem,* Cwichelm I *108.*

Cynegyls, Kynegyls, I 108; *m.a-stem,* Cynegils I 101, etc.

Denisc, *adj.* DANISH II 25.

Dorcanceaster, *f.ō-stem,* Dorchester-on-Thames (Oxon.) I 113n.

Dūnstan, *m.a-stem,* (St) Dunstan II 3, III 381n, etc.

Ēadgar, *m.a-stem,* (King) Edgar III 1n, 112, 371, etc.

Ēadmund, *m.a-stem,* (St) Edmund II 5, 14, 41, etc.

Ēadwine, *m.i-stem,* (King) Edwin I 6n, 92, 126.

Ēadzige, *nom.* III 23, 36; **Ēadsige,** *nom.* III 69; **Ēadzies,** *gen.* III 63; *m.i-stem,* Eadsige.

Eald Mynster, *n.a-stem,* the Old Minster (Winchester) I 118n, III 23, 97, 199.

Ēastengle, *m.i-stem pl.* the East Angles, East Anglia II 14, 33.

Eferwic, *n.a-stem,* YORK I 91.

Ēlig, *as f.jō-stem,* Ely II 216.

Engle, *m.i-stem pl.* [ANGLE³]; the English I 1, etc.

Englisc, *adj.* ENGLISH; *as sb.* the English language I 33, II 10.

Francland, *n.a-stem,* [FRANK *sb.*¹ + LAND]; the land of the Franks I 198.

Glēawceaster, *f.ō-stem,* Gloucester I 234.

Gregorius, *nom.* (St) Gregory II 198n.

118

Hāmtūnscīr, *f.ō-stem*, Hampshire III 12.

Hædde,*m.ja-stem*, Hædde I 117n.

Heofonfeld, *m.u-stem*, Heavenfield I 32n.

Hinguar, **Hingwar**, *m.a-stem*, Ingwar II 28n, 31, etc.

Honorius, I *103*n.

Hubba, *m.n-stem*, Ubba II 28n, 31.

Īrland, *n.a-stem*, Ireland I 198, 200.

Iūdei, *nom.pl.* the Jews II 222.

Iūdeisc, *adj.* [JUDEISH]; *JEWISH*; *pl. as sb.* the Jews II 90, III 310*, 364n.

Iudoc, *m.a-stem*, (St) Judoc III 96n.

Kynegyls, see **Cynegyls**.

Landferð, *m.a-stem*, Landferth III 334n.

Laurentię, *dat.* (St) Lawrence II 199n.

Læden,*n.a-stem*, [LEDEN]; Latin III 335n.

Lēofstan, *m.a-stem*, Leofstan II 192n.

Lindesig, *as f.jō-stem*, Lindsey I 148n.

Lindisfarnea, *gen.sg.* the island of Lindisfarne I 140n.

Maserfeld, *m.u-stem*, Oswestry (Salop.) I 129n.

Myrce; **Myrcena**, *gen.* I 125, etc; **Myrcan**, *dat.* I 147n; *m.i-stem pl.* the Mercians, Mercia.

Nīwe Mynster, *n.a-stem*, the New Minster (Winchester) III 95n.

Nor(ð)hymbre, *m.i-stem pl.* the Northumbrians I 2, 58, etc.

Norðhymbre, *adj.* Northumbrian I 9.

Norðhymbrisc, *adj.* Northumbrian I 56.

Ōswig, *m.* (*orig. wa-stem?*), Oswi(u), Osweo I 137n.

Ōswold, *m.a-stem*, (St) Oswald I 2, 10, 11, etc.

Ōswyn,*f.jō- or i-stem*, Oswyn II 158.

Paulus, *nom.* (St) Paul III 311.

Penda, *m.n-stem*, Penda I 125, 127n.

Peohtas, see **Piht**.

Petre, *dat.* II 89, **Petres**, *gen.* I 144, III 117; (St) Peter.

Piht; **Peohtas**, *nom.pl.* I 88; *m.a-stem*, PICT.

Rōm, *f.* ROME I 103, III 162, etc.

Rōmanisc, *adj.* [ROMANISH]; Roman; *as sb.* I 33.

Rōmeburh, *f.athem.stem*, Rome I 100, II 199.

Scotland, *n.a-stem*, Scotland I 4n, 39.

Scot(t), *m.a-stem*, SCOT[1] I 89, III 376.

Scyttysc, *adj. as sb.* [SCOTTISH]; Gaelic I 55.

Sebastianus, *nom.* (St) Sebastian II 101n.

Swiðun, **Swyðun**, *m.a-stem*, (St) Swithin III 4, 11, 20, etc.

þēodred, *m.a-stem*, Theodred II 163n, 186.

Westse(a)xe, *or* -se(a)xan; **Westsexena**, *gen.* I 101n, 102n, II 34; **Westseaxan**,*dat.* I 107n; *m.i- or n-stem pl.* the West Saxons, Wessex.

Wihtland, *n.a-stem*, the Isle of Wight III 129, 281, 329.

Winceaster, *f.ō-stem*, Winchester (Hants.) III 12, 84, 151, etc.

Wincelcumb, *m.a-stem*, Winchcombe (Gloucs.?) III 28.

Wintanceaster, *f.ō-stem*, Winchester (Hants.) I 117.

Printed and bound by CPI Group (UK) Ltd, Croydon, CR0 4YY

13/04/2025

14656587-0001